Arkansas
Pie

Arkansas

A DELICIOUS slice *of the* NATURAL STATE

Pie

KAT ROBINSON

photography by
KAT ROBINSON & GRAV WELDON

AMERICAN PALATE

Published by American Palate
A Division of The History Press
Charleston, SC 29403
www.historypress.net

First published 2012
Second printing 2013

Manufactured in the United States

ISBN 978.1.60949.876.4

Library of Congress Cataloging-in-Publication Data

Robinson, Kat.
Arkansas pie : a delicious slice of the Natural State / Kat Robinson ; photography by Kat
Robinson and Grav Weldon.
pages cm
Includes index.
ISBN 978-1-60949-876-4
1. Pies--Arkansas. 2. Restaurants--Arkansas. 3. Bakeries--Arkansas. 4. Arkansas--
Description and travel. 5. Robinson, Kat--Travel--Arkansas. 6. Arkansas--History, Local. 7.
Arkansas--Social life and customs. I. Weldon, Grav. II. Title.
TX773.R622 2012
641.86'5209767--dc23
2012044162

To Kitty Waldon
my mom, who's put up with decades of oddity from me

For Hunter Robinson
my daughter, who will probably cause the same sort of havoc

Contents

Contents

VII. The Case for Possum Pie

An asterisk (*) denotes a listing that contains a pie recipe.

Foreword

If I'm hungry and I'm in Arkansas, I let Kat Robinson tell me where to eat. I'd be a fool not to.

Over the years we've known each other, Kat and I have pushed a lot of food around on our plates, from stuff we've cooked ourselves to medieval feasts fit for kings and queens. That's a lot of calories under the bridge, and I have grown to respect Kat's sharp intellect regarding culinary matters. Not only does she know her herbs from her spices, she knows how to coax the most out of every ingredient. And she isn't afraid to give a frank, after-meal postmortem to account for the successes and failures of each individual dish—even if she'd cooked them herself.

That kind of humble self-realization does a cook well, and it does a food writer even better. It means that Kat knows what's important: good ingredients put together the right way to make the best food possible. That may mean adhering to the tenets of tradition and not changing Great-Grandma's biscuit recipe by one iota, and it may mean using your favorite cookbook as a mere framework upon which you improvise your way to a dish that barely resembles the original intent. After all, cooking is where the end truly justifies the means, and the only acceptable end is flavor.

What's that you say? Presentation? Gentle Reader, if how your food looks is anywhere near as important to you as how it tastes, then I must suggest you're doing this whole eating thing wrong.

So: pie. As I once opined in a magazine column, "Cakes are for occasions; pies are just because." That, to me, captures what is so essentially special

Apple pie at Betty's Steaks and Chicken in Harrisburg. *Kat Robinson.*

about pie: it has no season, it needs no reason. It can be plain or fancy or easy or complex, and no one will judge you the harsher because it was one but not t'other. Give someone a pie and you are giving them love, and they will love you right back.

Pie is always proper. Somewhere in the myriad permutations of the form is one that will make the perfect ending to whatever meal you're serving. And to tell the truth, even if you pick one that isn't a complete culinary match, nobody's going to complain. It's pie, for crying out loud!

So rejoice! This book that you're smart enough to be holding is your ticket to pie nirvana in the natural state. Kat has done all the hard work for you, clocking the miles and finding every last nook and/or cranny where pie is to be had in Arkansas.

Strawberry rhubarb pie a la mode at the Village Wheel in Bull Shoals. *Kat Robinson.*

But this is no mere listing—uh-uh, nosiree. It's the map for a pilgrimage to every pie shrine in this unique, quirky, mysterious little state. And she doesn't skimp on the narrative either. In addition to sharing the stories of those folks who make and sell pies, as well as some of her own experiences, Kat lays before you a vivid, enticing image of every slice and slab in language that'll have you licking your fingers…and quite possibly the pages.

Take her description of the Village Wheel restaurant's strawberry rhubarb pie. Normally if I saw either a strawberry or a rhubarb on a plate, I wouldn't touch it. But Kat's account of this particular pie is so poetically beautiful that the moment I read it, I had to fight off an urge to drive to Bull Shoals right away for a slice.

You, too, will experience this response as you peruse the pages and your eyes start feeding cues to your other senses. You'll smell the crusts being blind-baked, feel the fork drag through thick custard, taste the chocolate, the fruit, the nuts, the meringue…

Dangit, Kat, now I'm all hungry for pie again! Be ready to go in fifteen minutes—I'll buy if you'll navigate.

Eric Francis
September 2012
North Little Rock, Arkansas

Introduction

*J*elly pie. *The heck is jelly pie?*

That was my reaction to seeing a map produced by the ICanHasCheezburger.com folks and picked up by the popular food blog Serious Eats in early 2011. The map took each of the fifty states and correlated them with a popular dish in that state.

Except…Arkansas was identified with a dish called jelly pie. I've lived in Arkansas my whole life. Both sides of my family have been in Arkansas for generations. And I had never, *never* heard of jelly pie.

I called my mom. I called friends. I posted on Facebook and asked questions on Twitter. I even mentioned it in a radio appearance. No one I knew or corresponded with had ever heard of it. I went back to the original post on the ICanHasCheezburger.com website and commented thusly:

> *I absolutely have to correct this.*
>
> *Being a lifelong Arkansawyer, I heard the term "jelly pie" TODAY. I'm now doing a search on it to see what can be done to fix this misconception.*
>
> *It's true, Arkansas has no official state food. But there are foods that originate here. We host the Hope Watermelon Festival which claims the world's largest melons and the Cave City Watermelon Festival that serves up the (academically asserted) world's sweetest melons. We produce a fantastic amount of rice and soybeans.*
>
> *Cheese dip was invented here in the 40s. The cheese-filled hot dog is one of our inventions. We love sassafras tea and rice smothered in chicken gravy*

(and rice with just sugar and butter to boot). Our state produces fabulous cheese straws, funnel cake mix, yellow corn grits and muscadine wine.

We like our pies—oh heavens we do—but we prefer them meringued or creamed or with a little coconut in them. We also love our burgers, having an almost unreasonable number of burger offerings around these parts.

Our cultural food oddity is the Reuben sandwich, found on about 90 percent of non-ethnic menus here and traced back to the first days of Oaklawn Racing Park in Hot Springs. We're used to picking blackberry seeds from between our teeth in summer and enjoying our Arkansas Black apples in the winter.

If you really do have any questions about Arkansas, its food, its culture and cuisine, drop me a line at kat@tiedyetravels.com. I stand behind this answer 100 percent.

I had, at the time, just completed a quick article for Serious Eats entitled "The 15 Best Pies in Arkansas." I wrote my editors there and bitterly complained. I also complained to fellow Arkansans and mentioned to my boss at the *Arkansas Times*, Max Brantley, that I knew a lot about pie in Arkansas and had never heard of this jelly pie.

I didn't realize then that pie was about to become a significant part of my life.

At the time, I was writing "Eat Arkansas," the blog for food lovers for the *Arkansas Times*. I was also writing "Tie Dye Travels," my own travel blog that had taken off and grown Internet-style wings. I had my Serious Eats cred and my Lonely Planet cred and was contributing to whomever wanted to pick up my stuff, be it *Times* competitor *Sync Weekly* (though not on food) or *Food Network Magazine* or *Arkansas Wild*. I was traveling a lot too.

I'd started up an "Eat Arkansas" feature called "Pieday," where each week I'd share a pie from around the state and talk about where it was from. The groundwork had been set. I found myself scanning menus and questioning waitresses over desserts. I always had my camera out, and I took notes on anything that came on a crust.

Around June that year, Max asked me to start working on my next cover piece, a Thanksgiving week piece on…you guessed it, pie. My other two cover stories (on Arkansas food gifts and the best breakfasts in the state) had also appeared in this spot on the calendar in previous years, and I knew the sort of research I'd have to undertake.

But it wasn't that easy. I suppose in some states a restaurant might be like as not to have pie. Here in Arkansas, we love pie. We love its infinite

Raspberry cream cheese pie at Trio's in Little Rock. *Kat Robinson*.

diversity and its infinite combinations (to paraphrase the old Vulcan maxim). We claim so many varieties that the head swivels.

In Arkansas around the holidays, pecan pie is so prevalent that a dinner table is empty without one. Feuds have broken out over the superiority between sweet potato and pumpkin pie. Restaurants compete over which has the tallest meringue on its coconut or chocolate pies, and you can tell the progressing weeks of summer based on what pie shows up at Sunday dinner.

Our oldest and most famous restaurants, for the most part, are known for their pies. Every innovative young chef seems to have a special one. Almost every drive-in, diner, family-style restaurant and soul food shack has its own version, and it's nary a barbecue restaurant that doesn't have a grand fried pie. You can even find good pie in Chinese restaurants, at service stations and inside flea markets and antique stores. Pie is everywhere in Arkansas.

Before the year was out, I'd eaten bites of at least 173 different Arkansas pies. I chronicled the best I found in the *Times* article, citing the top 100 slices. But even as that article headed to print, I knew I hadn't done it all. There were still more places for me to try.

I took a few months off from my pie research, trying just one in a restaurant in all of December 2011 and January 2012 (the excellent and irresistible grasshopper pie at Club 178 in Bull Shoals). And I left the tough world of freelancing to take a demanding but long-desired job with the Arkansas Department of Parks and Tourism.

But I was still curious about the pie idea. I had mapped out all the places where I'd found good pie in Arkansas, and there were spaces I had missed, particularly across north central Arkansas and the Delta. I kept receiving recommendations, too.

And then it was summer, and Will McKay with The History Press contacted me about writing books about Arkansas food. There were a few ideas pitched around, but the subject that lured me the most was this one. I wanted to delve more into the pies of Arkansas, write more of the stories surrounding these sweet delights and share the variations with others.

It has required a lot more travel and sampling than you might imagine. I could have just listed places people recommended to me, but I felt it was important that I reach these different environments and sample these pies. And in case you were wondering, there were few slices I actually consumed in a single setting. On research days (usually weekends, as to not conflict with my day job), I'd be up early in the morning and traveling, and by the end of my travels, I would have sampled anywhere from four to nine pies. The regular routine was to photograph the tar out of the pie, take a bite or two and then request a box to take the rest home. Those pies were usually cycled among my friends for consumption. There was one weekend where over a thirty-six-hour period, my photographer and I checked in at twenty-two different pie locations. We ended up with more than a dozen pies worthy of inclusion in the book…but we had to try them all.

The best ones? They're the ones I craved days and even months later, the ones that came to me in my dreams. The stories affected me similarly. I found myself sharing them with others I encountered. And those stories include a little more, too. Some of the locations, some of the pies resurrected memories. Some of the research was entertaining. There are a lot of bits of my life wrapped up in this book.

What's next? I haven't a clue. Whatever the future holds, I have a feeling that Arkansas food will be involved, and that won't be a bad thing.

And I never did find a jelly pie, though there was a lady down at Historic Washington State Park who found a recipe in a cookbook from way back. Considering how many different types of pie I did discover, that's saying something.

Variations on a Theme of Pies

What is a pie? That's something for consideration. After all, there are many different sorts of pie and a lot of things that seem pie-like. For the purposes of this book, I chose to focus on sweet pies rather than savory pies—partly because that's what most folks are talking about when they discuss Arkansas pie and partly because the research woulda killed me.

What I came up with was this.

- A pie has a crust. Whether it's a simple flour and water crust, a graham cracker crust or even some strange blend of saltines and meringue, it's present.
- The pie *needs* the crust. This is what differentiates pie from cheesecake. A cheesecake can theoretically be made sans crust and usually only comes with a bottom crust. With the exception of some casserole pies (see possum pie), some form of crust is absolutely critical to containment.

I did debate on whether fried pies should be included. In the end, they came along for the ride, mostly because of the culture of the hand pie, a convenience food that often incorporates the exact sort of filling normally obtained in a regular pie but needing to be convenient to the working class, especially truckers and farmers and the like who should be able to carry and consume their dessert with a single hand.

Apple lattice pie at Catalpa General Store. *Grav Weldon*.

Within those definitions, there are several variations on pies:

- FRUIT PIES. These are pies that contain fruit or a fruit puree over a crust, usually topped with a solid or lattice top. This includes apple, peach, blueberry, blackberry, cherry and other similar pies. This sort of pie is always baked.
- CREAM PIES. These are pies that contain a custard layer topped by a thick layer of whipped cream or Cool-Whip. These include coconut cream, banana cream, lemon cream and chocolate cream pies. They can be baked or not; the crust is usually a crushed cookie crust of some sort. Possum pies fit in this category.
- FRUIT CREAM PIES. These are pies with a fruit filling and a cream top. Fresh strawberry pies are the most common example.
- CREAM CHEESE PIES. These are pies that contain a layer of cream cheese filling on the bottom, usually sweetened with sugar and often tarted up with lemon juice. Cherry cream cheese pies are the most common example, but strawberry and peach variations are widespread during their associated growing seasons. These pies are rarely baked.

- Nut pies. These are pies that consist of a nut (pecan, walnut, macadamia nut) that have been made into a custard involving eggs that becomes a "goo" forming the heart of the pie. These pies are always baked.
- Meringue pies. These are baked pies that contain a pastry layer on the bottom, rich custard in the middle (usually coconut, chocolate, caramel, butterscotch or lemon) and a fluffy layer of egg white meringue on top.
- Chocolate pies. These pies contain chocolate and may or may not include a cream layer. Most chocolate pies are baked.
- Icebox pies. These pies usually consist of whipped cream beaten into a flavoring agent of some sort, poured into a crushed cookie shell and sometimes topped with another ingredient. These pies are never baked and must be stored at or below forty degrees.
- Frozen pies. Similar to icebox pies but stored below thirty-two degrees.
- Combination pies. Any pie that combines two or more other types of pie. For instance, the PCP at Ed and Kay's Restaurant combines a nut pie (pecan) with a fruit pie (pineapple) and adds coconut. The cherry cream cheese meringue pie at Hillbilly Hideout is a combination of a meringue pie and a cream cheese pie.

Of course, there are exceptions to everything (see the hot fudge pie at Big John's Shake Shack). And then there are fried pies, which break down into their own categories:

- Fruit fried pies
- Nut fried pies
- Cream fried pies
- Chocolate fried pies

And when it comes to crusts, there are even further divisions:

- Flour and water crust
- Flour and butter crust
- Sandy bottom crust (flour plus pecans)
- Crushed cookie crust
- Graham cracker crust
- Unusual crusts (for instance, the pressed coconut crust of the peach cream cheese pie at Katherine's Café Amore)

Once you tally in all these factors, the endless variations follow.

Pies on the line at Franke's Cafeteria on Rodney Parham. *Grav Weldon*.

PART I

The Pies of Legend

Known for generations, these are the pies that your grandparents still talk about.

The Cliff House Inn

The best-known pie

Scenic Highway 7 used to have a whole lot of traffic, especially the stretch from Russellville up to Harrison. That was the way to Dogpatch USA when I was a kid, and you passed all sorts of great stuff like stunning Buffalo National River vistas, gift shops, rock shops and Booger Hollow. There was this place right below Jasper on Scenic 7 that looked out over what always seemed like the greenest part of the valley. This was and still is the Cliff House Inn, a small restaurant, gift shop and bed-and-breakfast perched over what we call the Arkansas Grand Canyon.

Opened in 1967, the place has seen its share of owners. Among them were Bob and Francis McDaniel, who owned the Cliff House Inn for about eighteen years. Francis wanted a couple of things for the restaurant there: a signature biscuit and a signature pie.

I talked with Becky McLaurin, one of the current owners, and she told me this: "Francis tried different pies and hit on it, because people would call ahead and ask, 'You know that pie you make? The one with the pineapple? We're heading that way and wanted to make sure you had it.'" Hence the name of the pie she stuck with: Company's Comin' Pie.

It's not like any other sort of pie you've had, or at least I am guessing not since I haven't. It's the crust that's the difference. "The pie crust is sorta like a Divinity crust," McLaurin told me, "made with egg whites and sugar. It takes about an hour to make a pie crust. You beat the egg whites and

Company's Comin' Pie at the Cliff House Inn near Jasper. *Chuck Haralson/Arkansas Department of Parks and Tourism (ADPT).*

the sugar for about twenty-five minutes, and then you add crushed saltine crackers and a cup of pecan pieces, and then you stir that in and it's kinda like a thick gooey mixture. You take and divide it into two pie tins. You form the crust with a spatula and bake it for twenty-five minutes.

"When you get ready to serve a pie, you take a pint of real whipping cream and put a little sugar in, and then you add a bit of crushed pineapple. Fill your pie crust with that. It's kind of an unusual pie, but people love it."

It's certainly unusual, and its name caught the attention of folks who work in tourism (like I do today). The McDaniels sold the restaurant to Jim Berry, who was very active in the tourism community. Then 1986 came along (the year of Arkansas' sesquicentennial) and there was a campaign going on, "Company's Comin', Let's Get Ready." The suggestion was made to have the pie at the Cliff House Inn named the state pie of Arkansas.

Here's where the story gets a little strange. See, Mrs. McLaurin shared with me that the Arkansas General Assembly made it the official state pie of Arkansas. But it's not listed anywhere. I've been on a hunt for that information, and I still haven't been able to nail it down. Regardless, the Company's Comin' Pie has been listed in all sorts of places as the state's pie,

Then-governor Bill Clinton receives his very own Company's Comin' Pie. *ADPT*.

and the recipe pops up now and again in Arkansas cookbook compilations. That, at least, is no secret.

Dogpatch USA, Booger Hollow and the rock shops may have dried up and moved on, but the Cliff House Inn is still open for business. And yes, you can have yourself a slice of pie. Be sure to say hello to owners Bob and Becky McLaurin if you get the chance. You'll find the place south of Jasper a few miles on Scenic Highway 7. Call (870) 446-2292 or check out the website.

Company's Comin' Pie

6 egg whites

1 teaspoon cream of tartar

2 cups sugar

1 teaspoon vanilla

1 sleeve saltine crackers, crushed

½ cup chopped pecans

TOPPING:

1 small container whipped topping

3 tablespoons sugar

2 tablespoons crushed pineapple

Beat egg whites until fluffy. Add cream of tartar and sugar. Beat 25 minutes or until stiff. Stir in vanilla. Stir in crackers and pecans by hand.

Spray two pie pans with nonstick spray. Divide mixture evenly between pans. Spread mixture in pan, forming a crust. Bake at 285° for 25 minutes or until done. Combine topping ingredients. Pour into pie shell. Serve and enjoy.

Franke's Cafeteria

Cinnamon cream pie—rich and layered, like its history

Arkansas' oldest continually operating restaurant isn't a barbecue shack, a hamburger joint or even a steak place. It's a cafeteria. That may sound pedestrian, especially in this age of Luby's and Ryan's and those sorts. But when you're talking about Franke's, you're not talking about institutional food. You're talking about some of the finest Arkansas cuisine to grace a menu.

Franke's didn't start out as a cafeteria. It was first a bakery, sort of a hole-in-the-wall joint that served up doughnuts and such in downtown Little Rock, when it was started in 1919 by C.A. Franke. Five years later, the first cafeteria under the name was opened at what's now Capital Avenue between Main and Louisiana Streets.

There were other locations. The one I remember from my youth was in University Mall next to Osco Drug, across from Montgomery Ward's. It was there from before I was born until right before the mall was sold off and demolished. I can remember standing in the Nut Hut and looking across through the windows at all the diners in the dark wood-paneled and curtained dining room, thinking how fancy everyone was.

There is still a location downstairs in the downtown Regions Bank building; during the times in my life when I worked temp jobs to supplement my fledgling radio career, I'd grab my tray and join the masses, picking up roast beef and peas and egg custard pie to consume before returning to the drudgery of my day.

These days, though, there's no University Mall, and I tend to haunt West Little Rock more than downtown. Which is fine, since there's a Franke's on Rodney Parham Road in the Market Street Shopping Center. From the exterior, it's unimposing; inside, it's well appointed and clean, just as fancy if not fancier than most of your mid-range restaurants. And best of all, it's reverently quiet.

It's still a cafeteria, not a buffet. You head to the end of the line, grab a tray and cloth-wrapped utensils and choose the dishes you would like with the help of smartly attired attendants. In the salad section alone you could get lost without a guide. Sure, there's the traditional restaurant-style lettuce and cucumber and tomato salad with dressing; there are also a plethora of Arkansas-friendly salads—carrot salad; marinated salad with onions, tomatoes and cucumbers (strangely similar to Indian kachumber salad); black-eyed pea and pepper salad; Ambrosia salad; green bean salad; pea salad and at least six types of congealed salad. There are beets and peaches and okra of varying sorts.

Entrées vary by the day, but there's usually always roast beef, ham, fried chicken, roasted chicken and hamburger steak. I've seen chicken croquettes, baked catfish, fried catfish, pepper steak with onions, cabbage rolls and pork chops. There are more sides than you can shake a stick at: cabbage with ham, green beans with bacon, corn in oh so many preparations, rice, mashed potatoes, fried potatoes, umpteen types of beans and peas, carrots, mac and cheese—and if you're really lucky, sweet potato casserole. Or even better, eggplant casserole. There are white bread rolls, wheat bread rolls, regular cornbread and jalapeño cornbread full of corn and pepper bits.

And then there's pie. The one thing that about 95 percent of all Arkansas restaurants I have visited share is some variation on pie—fried, meringue, cream, fruit, whatever. Franke's has more pie than you can shake a spoon at, more than you can eat in a week, more than you can conceive of in a sweet luscious dream. I can almost close my eyes and count off what's in line in the case in almost always the same order: lemon meringue, pecan, sweet potato, brownie, custard and chocolate pecan on top and all the cobblers and cream pies on the bottom—banana, chocolate, coconut, Key lime, strawberry pie topped with whipped cream. Sometimes there's another sort here and there thrown in for good measure, seasonal pies like cherry or blueberry or such.

If there were ever an unheralded pie place in Little Rock, Franke's would be it. There are always at least a dozen different sorts of pie out and ready to go when you pass through the line. But there's one pie Franke's offers that I have seen nowhere else, outside the occasional family gathering. That amazing pie is the cinnamon cream.

Oh, certainly I have tried all the different sorts of pies. I do like the denseness of the brownie pie with its topping of marshmallows and the almost frothy coconut cream. The lemon meringue is perfectly formed and the pecan a smooth Karo-nut symphony of southern delight.

But that cinnamon cream is a house specialty. I have missed it a time or two—coming at dinner when Franke's has run out for the day. Any time that's happened, I've choked back my emotions and made another decent yet not quite as good choice.

If you've had it, you know what I mean. It's impossibly light, barely cloying and yet the most perfect representation of a cinnamon roll in any other medium I have come across. There are all the flavors, the cinnamon and nutmeg and butter, all delicately balanced and layered into a house-made shell. From the bottom up it's graham cracker, cinnamon, a sweet vanilla custard and cinnamon, a lighter custard and a frothy whipped cream and a little more cinnamon graham crumble on the top.

It might appear to be tiramisu-like. It is not. It might appear to be a cross between a banana pudding and banana cream pie. It is not. It is, in my mind, the best use of cinnamon in a pie shell. And I have yet to be able to replicate it perfectly.

That's why there have been times I've dropped in and passed through the line, past the congealed salads and the entrees and peas and such, just to get a piece of pie in a Styrofoam box to take home with me. It's a very special treat. It comes recommended.

I've been known to take guests from outside Arkansas to Franke's. It's fun to watch them. I guess they're expecting something closer to the retail buffet experience. I like to show them one of the many variations of Arkansas home cooking, with items such as eggplant casserole, corn pudding, PurpleHull peas and butter beans and jalapeño cornbread and marinated salad. Sometimes I even get some fresh tomato slices—I have to ask for those—so the meal can more properly emulate my southwest Arkansas roots.

And there's one more thing about Franke's: service doesn't end when you pass through the register section at the end of the tray line. A porter will come take your tray as soon as you sit down, so you're not left trying to find a place for it on your table. He'll even carry your tray for you if your hands are full or if you need help. A kind waiter will drive a cart by every once in a while with refills on coffee and tea and take-home boxes. Other waiters will check on your soft drink. And there is no rush. Take your time. Enjoy your conversation. You can pay up when you leave.

Franke's is a dining experience that's different from most others in Arkansas. Here's hoping it'll remain the oldest continually operating restaurant in the state for a long time.

Rhoda's Famous Hot Tamales

A delightful calling

For Rhoda Adams of Lake Village, pie making is a calling from God, and she shares her testimony with others. In 1973, she started selling the sweet potato pies she once made at home to others for the church.

"That's the only pie I knowed how to make, and that was sweet potato," she said, "and I'd sell all sorts of chips and candy and cupcakes, all that out of my house for the church, give all the money from what I sold to the church."

"Then somebody said, 'Do you make this kinda pie? That kinda pie?' and I had never made a pecan pie, and you may think I'm lying…I make pecan pie, folks walk up to my car and get my pecan pie and eat it before me and then they want a bunch of them."

A bunch? Well, yeah—because Adams's sweet potato and pecan pies and the other pies she generally makes are tiny three-inch-wide affairs in tiny little pie tins—the perfect size for a single dessert.

Delta travel writer (and my good friend) Kim Williams went down to Lake Village with Aristotle Interactive in the summer of 2012 to record a video of Adams working in her shop and sharing that testimony. We both love "Miss Rhoda." She is a Madea—a beloved mother who shares her love through her food. You can watch that video on Arkansas.com. To hear her go on about the pies, well…

"I make up a bunch of these pecan pies, and these half-and-half…oh, honey."

I have been in Adams's shop and stood in her kitchen watching the tamale operation. I learned a long time ago you don't get there late in the day because you might not have anything more to eat than chips and a Coke. She and her family will spend a whole day past midnight each week hand-rolling tamales, and when what she's cooked up is gone, it's gone—and so are the pies.

Now, you can order a big full-size pie from Miss Rhoda if you like. But if you're just dropping in for a hot plate lunch or a coffee can full of tamales, the little pies will do you just fine.

The day my photographer and I went to try to shoot those pies, we arrived around lunchtime and the joint was packed. The parking lot was packed. There were people sitting outside to eat and a line all the way out the door. That's how good those tamales are.

Those half-and-half pies were tempting, but I was curious and got myself a little tart of this, a little pie of that—the sweet potato and the pecan and the chocolate meringue, too. At a dollar a pie, it's a deal.

The chocolate meringue was a nice chocolate custard with a tacky meringue top, sticky and gooey in all the right ways but not fluffy like most meringues. It was tasty but still not the star of the show. That was tougher to determine.

The sweet potato pie has its own graces, and I know why. It's a firm, not-too-sweet made-from-the-real-deal pie with just a bit of fibrous potato left in the mix. There's no doubt you're eating a sweet potato pie when you bite into it. The crust is supple and buttery. The consistency is firm. The sweetness is measurable. It's a good, filling little pie.

But the real star was the pecan pie—a rich, deep-colored custard with a hint of butter and bourbon overtones. It's meaty and a little cloying, but for its size it's perfect, bigger than the pie shell goodness. There's a depth to each bite, that combination of good Karo-nut syrup and fresh shelled pecans. It's the not-to-be-missed star of the bunch. And to think that when she started out, Adams didn't know how to make pecan pie!

She has pie every day she's open, which is every day except Sunday. And there are so many varieties she makes. "I make coconut pies, chocolate pies, half coconut pies"—I am assuming she meant half coconut and half chocolate, which were on the counter—"lemon icebox, lemon meringue, pecan, sweet potato, fried peach, fried apple turnover. That's how He has blessed me, and I didn't know how to do that stuff until I obeyed Him."

And a good number of days she's out in her white SUV with the hand-lettered sign taped to the side, cruising around one of the RV parks alongside Lake Chicot. She sells those little pies right out of the vehicle, along with coffee cans packed with two dozen tamales. The tamales are divine affairs

Rhoda Adams of Rhoda's Famous Hot Tamales. *Grav Weldon.*

made from beef, chicken fat, cornmeal and love. I have picked up those tamales too and eaten them at home and on road trips and once on the side of I-20 while stopped for hours because of a bridge collision in Vicksburg. She gives you a fork to go with it, and if you only get a dozen, they're wrapped twice in aluminum foil and once in a paper bag, but you are still going to get tamale juice everywhere. I usually end up eating mine right out of the shuck.

Nearly forty years, and "Miss Rhoda" is still going strong, feeding hungry people and sharing her strong faith. "I don't give myself no credit on nothin'. My auntie got me started on the hot tamales, and the Lord got me started on the pies and give us stuff like that, and I go out in my car and have so many chips and pies and different things, and you see the children buying the cupcakes and the different stuff and the schoolhouse buys my stuff and sells them at school. So I have been blessed."

Ed and Kay's Restaurant

Ed and Kay's Restaurant serves up memories on a plate.

For more than fifty years, Ed and Kay's has been serving up hot breakfasts, filling lunches and great pies in Benton. It's been in the southernmost Benton curve of I-30 so long that I can't remember it not being there (well, I'm not over fifty, so that makes sense), and I've seen a lot of good meals there. I've also had a great deal of fun there.

The place started out as Ed and Alma's, and Miss Alma made all those pies. When Ed died in the mid-1970s, Alma kept it going. She sold it to the Diemers in 1982 and retired. They renamed it Ed and Kay's Restaurant, and that's what it's been ever since.

Back when I was a television producer, we sent our morning show down to the shop. It was 2006. I can quite clearly recall Kay Diemer telling tales to one of my lead anchors, B.J. Sams, and how one of the pie ladies showed my other lead anchor, Robyn Richardson, how to make that fabulous meringue. I also remember Robyn licked the meringue off a spatula—but I won't share with you the reaction of a certain pair of television directors over that particular activity.

Pie's what convinced me to send the show down there in the first place. You'd be hard-pressed to find a taller pie in the state of Arkansas. The meringue is piled thick and richly on coconut and chocolate meringue pies. They've become so famous that some people only know Ed and Kay's as "the Mile-High Pie shop." And I can see why they say that. It's almost a daily

Ed and Kay's Restaurant in Benton. *Grav Weldon.*

contest with the folks who work there to see if they can manage to squeeze even a millimeter more in height out of the meringue. It's a thick foam, rising four to six inches above the custard. It is impressive.

I know it may sound strange, but while the meringue pies are fabulous, they're not the one that steals my heart and money from my wallet every visit.

I like going to Ed and Kay's for breakfast. I've had a great number of the breakfasts offered there, but the best one I have ever had was the one I shared with seven of my friends. We were all about to head down to Louisiana for a wedding, and everyone ordered something different. My friend Terri ordered the Kitchen Sink Omelet, just for the heck of it. It's not really called that, but it might as well be. It's listed as "Any or All" under the omelet section of the menu, and it's $9.80. It includes (if you want it all) ham, bacon and sausage; cheddar, pepper jack, American and Swiss cheeses; onions, green bell peppers, black olives, tomatoes, mushrooms and jalapeños. It's served up with a bowl of cream gravy, fried potatoes and a choice of a pancake, toast or biscuit. It is a remarkably huge and colorful meal. She didn't finish it. Her husband, Jerry, who had already polished his plate, couldn't finish her omelet either. It's just massive.

Me? When I go for breakfast, I usually go for the chicken fried steak combo breakfast ($7.80 with two eggs). It's a nice crispy piece of tenderized beef covered in cream gravy. I usually get mine with a little extra gravy on the side. The made-from-scratch cream gravy is great on one of Ed and Kay's fluffy biscuits; I usually take home a biscuit half with gravy to savor later.

What never does make it home are the fried potatoes. They're available with any meal, and they're decadent—julienne-style red potatoes with black pepper and herbs cooked up in butter. Oh, man. Some of my dining companions have chosen to doctor theirs up with ketchup and the like. I prefer mine as they are. So does my daughter Hunter, who has loved getting her hands on them since the first time she had them.

There's also lunch and dinner, including a special every day. I've had the hot roast beef before, smothered in brown gravy and served up with fried squash and macaroni and cheese. One thing I can always guarantee when I go to Ed and Kay's, and that's a lot of food. Side items that swamp the plate. Hot rolls or corn bread with every noontime meal. Generous entrée portions. It's just good hospitality.

I've been taking Hunter since she was pretty small, and I still take her from time to time. One of the waitresses always gets us set up there immediately with milk in a capped cup, even before we order. Hunter almost always gets the kid's vegetable plate—and it's always more food than she can eat in a sitting, which is saying something.

Now this is where I get back to the pie. From time to time, Ed and Kay's will run a dinnertime special: meals after 3:00 p.m. come with a free slice of pie. Doesn't matter, I order pie anyway. And usually it's not the

PCP Pie at Ed and Kay's Restaurant. *Kat Robinson*.

coconut or chocolate meringue, nor the lemon meringue or German chocolate or fudge. I order the PCP—a pie that's so good that…well. It's one of the best pies I've ever had. It's pineapple, coconut and pecan. It's created like a pecan pie but with a pineapple-pecan custard and coconut baked right into the top and crust. It's a best-of-everything pie, and I can't recommend it highly enough.

A fifty-year-old diner's a pretty amazing thing, and if it goes on another fifty years, it'll be even more amazing. I just hope it's there long enough for Hunter to take her daughter (should she have one) when she gets to be my age. It's just one of those Arkansas sort of places you can't keep passing up.

Now here's a treat for you: Miss Alma's original pie recipe!

PCP Pie a la Miss Alma

2 cups sugar
1 tablespoon cornmeal
1 tablespoon flour
5 eggs
pinch of salt
1 cup pecans, coarsely chopped
1 cup drained crushed pineapple
1 cup flaked coconut
1 stick butter, melted
1 blind-baked pie shell

Beat the sugar, cornmeal, flour, eggs and salt together. Stir in the pecans, pineapple and coconut. Stir in the melted butter and mix well. Bake at 300° in an unbaked pie shell approximately 45 to 60 minutes or until the pie is set. (You may need to cover the edges of the pie crust with foil or with a crust guard before the pie filling is completely cooked.)

Bulldog Restaurant

Bald Knob is a familiar crossroads to anyone who takes to exploring northeast Arkansas. From there, you can head out in any of the cardinal directions and hit another big town along the way: Batesville, Newport, Searcy—names that you become familiar with when exploring the U.S. 67 corridor.

A lot of folks were introduced to Bald Knob in the spring of 2011, when rising waters along the White River basin forced the closure of I-40. Instead of the regular route, drivers were sent along Highway 64 to Bald Knob, where they boarded U.S. 67/167 and went south to rejoin the interstate. The Bulldog Restaurant is not far from this intersection—maybe a block and a half. It's been around for more than forty years serving travelers and locals alike. It's known for its strawberry shortcake and its juicy square-patty burgers. There's always someone in line when you get there, and the tables are often packed.

The unheralded bit-player at the restaurant is often seen perched on the window between the kitchen and the front counter: a toasted meringue pie worthy of another look. It's coconut. It's a not-too-sweet custard between bubbly toasted coconut-infused meringue and a lightly blind-baked flour crust. While the meringue borders on the eggy side, it happens to also be very airy and light. The custard is heavy on the coconut flavor but more cream-like and dotted with flakes rather than a packing of flakes with a little cream.

You'll find the Bulldog Restaurant east off Exit 55 at Bald Knob. It's up on the hill on the left once you leave the highway.

Sim's Bar-B-Que

The very first barbecue I can clearly remember came in a paper boat wrapped tight in two layers of aluminum foil, with a stack of white bread wrapped in wax paper, all in a brown paper bag. The sauce was tangy and thin, and it left an indelible mark on my tongue.

That flavor, that scent and that experience were all part of growing up, whether it was my mom picking up a pound for a weekday dinner or grabbing a sandwich while out on Geyer Springs Road. It's the flavor of a slice of white bread that's been used to mop the last of that thin sauce out of the bottom of that aluminum foil. It's the flavor of Sim's Bar-B-Que.

Allen and Amelia Sims started the place back in 1937. It wasn't much, just meat, sauce, white bread and later beans. Eventually they sold to Ron Settlers, who incorporated the business. And it grew. It grew from Thirty-third Street to Barrow Road to Geyer Springs Road, with locations that have popped up from time to time elsewhere, like at Alltel Arena (now Verizon Arena) when it first opened.

The locations thrive for the same reason I still visit. That flavor, unlike any other Arkansas barbecue joint's sauce, is unique. It's just a few herbs and some sweetener, I am told, but it's more than that and everyone knows it. It's thin like Carolina barbecue but sweet instead of bitter, a strong flavor of vinegar throughout. And when no one is looking, when the meat is gone from that aluminum foil, I have been known to lick the package clean.

I even stuck to that flavor in high school. Sim's happened to be at the time the closest restaurant to Parkview Arts Magnet, and once I learned to drive, I became a regular.

I'm a long way past childhood, and Sim's is a long way past its beginnings, but it's still around and still going strong. I'd get my sandwich with slaw, as God intended, on the white bread rather than paying extra for a bun. Walking in today, more than twenty years after my graduation, the place is the same—except now there are plaques from some of the guys I went to school with, former Parkview Patriots who became Arkansas Razorbacks and a few of whom went on to the NBA. There's a photo there from Air Force One and whatnot. And the preferred brew for the average diner seems to be sweet tea or a cold Miller Lite.

Like everything else Sim's does, the recipe for the sweet potato pie they offer is a secret. I know it's made by Percy Walker, who has the Barrow Road location of which I speak. Now, I have had more than my share of sweet potato pies over the years, but this one is different. It's spicy. That's right. It has a whole lot of spice to it. It eats like a savory pie almost, with just enough sweetness to call it dessert. Smooth as custard. And it's not dolled up with whipped cream or ice cream or any of that nonsense. This pie stands on its own.

At the time of this writing, there are three Sim's Bar-B-Que locations: 2415 Broadway in downtown Little Rock, 7601 Geyer Springs in southwest Little Rock and the one at 1307 John Barrow Road, next to Shipley's Donuts and up the road from my alma mater. Get you some.

Colonial Steakhouse

The Pine Bluff mainstay's black bottom pie could be the most alcoholic slice in Arkansas.

Remember fruitcakes? Each Christmas, there'd be a fruitcake, heavy with rum, brought from one house to another. Johnny Carson used to joke about those fruitcakes and alluded to the fact that there were probably only a few fruitcakes that were passed from one person to another over the years.

I always wondered about those fruitcakes. The folks I knew who loved them most also almost always claimed that they were teetotalers, but they'd go back over and over again for slices of the rum-soaked goodness of fruitcake made from scratch. I also noticed these sorts of people never actually touched commercial fruitcake.

This is the sort of person, I believe, who'd love the old favorite of black bottom pie. The heavy pie used to be very popular with home cooks around these parts, but it's all but disappeared. I searched it out specifically, after my photographer asked about it, before he even came back to Arkansas to look for himself. More than three hundred restaurants later, there was nothing.

But my dear friend April Carter told me where I could find it. She grew up in Pine Bluff, and the Colonial Steakhouse was a favorite of her family's. It's even where she and her husband, Neale, had their wedding reception. She knew and recommended the restaurant's black bottom pie.

And what a pie. Between a creamy top and a dark chocolate bottom layer similar to that of a French silk pie lies thick, rum-laden custard. The scent

Colonial Steakhouse in Pine Bluff. *Grav Weldon.*

of it permeates the entire pie. It's a hefty pie, too, with a slice weighing as much as a large burger.

It's also extraordinarily rich. This one should be accompanied by a friend's fork and a cup of coffee to sober up with afterward.

The Village Wheel

Strawberry rhubarb—the perfect old-fashioned sweet-tart pie.

For more than thirty years, the Village Wheel in Bull Shoals has been making up several different desserts each day. This one's the best of the bunch.

The salty flour crust encapsulates slightly tart strawberries and even more tart rhubarb in a red glossy bath of just-sweet-enough sugar. The top crust is lightly sugar glazed. This pie deserves and requires a big honking scoop of vanilla ice cream.

Neal's Café

Pink. Old-fashioned in a very Lodge-meets-Automat sort of way. Wood-topped tables. Big deer and elk heads on the wall. A pie case on a counter in the center back of the room. Did I mention it is pink?

Neal's Café has been in operation since 1944 in the same little diner along U.S. 71B in Springdale. The Neal family has held it all that time. The

restaurant's motto is "Serving the Best of Better Foods." It's a time warp. A lovely, lovely time warp. And it's rumored to have fantastic pan-fried chicken, which is saying something since it's just a short jaunt down the street from the legendary AQ Chicken House.

Lemon meringue pie at Neal's Café in Springdale. *Kat Robinson.*

The pies, though. Tall toasted meringue pies kept under glass at the center back of the restaurant. From a distance it looks as if someone's piled meringue on top of Peeps…you know, those little marshmallow chicks you get at Easter? Well, they're not Peeps. The meringue is just applied thickly with tall whipped peaks that give a guide on how to cut the pies—one peak to a slice, six slices to a pie.

The tropical pie is recommended—a custardy blend of bananas, coconut and pineapple together. The lemon meringue is pungent. It's the deepest yellow you might ever contemplate, nuclear strong in both appearance and flavor. The translucent lemon curd has heft and substance, and it clings beautifully to the thick toasted meringue, all atop a folded flour and butter blind-baked crust.

You'll find Neal's Café on Thompson Street (U.S. 71B) behind the iconic sign.

Susan's Restaurant

Pie is available any time there's a pie in the cabinet—which is always at Susan's. There are chocolate and coconut meringues, cherry pie and whatever else happens to be available. For instance, in the spring Susan's offers a strawberry icebox pie made from fresh local strawberries blended into a whipped filling, poured into a graham cracker crust and topped with a few strawberries and then a thick layer of whipped cream. Susan's only uses fresh Arkansas strawberries for the pie, and when the

Strawberry icebox pie at Susan's Restaurant in Springdale. *Grav Weldon.*

strawberries are gone, the pie's gone too—to be replaced by a peach icebox pie made from Arkansas peaches. After that, it's blackberries. During months of the year when fresh fruit isn't available, Susan's does a fantastic peanut butter pie.

Also of note: Susan's is the sort of place where the waitresses still call you "sugar" and they'll touch your shoulder when they talk with you. You have been warned.

The Shangri-La Resort

Out on Lake Ouachita between Hot Springs and Mount Ida, there's a little peninsula with a little resort on it. The motor inn–style resort is something that's straight out of the 1950s, the sort of place you'd have gone to for a summer escape with the family. It's a place where the wind comes off the water and brings the temperature down ten or twenty degrees, where kids will play volleyball in the yard and where typical families with outboard motors on their johnboats will slide their trucks to the water's edge and push off for adventure.

It's also home to a little restaurant right off the lobby, a classic diner with paneling and fish on the walls and a series of picture windows, a short counter for the odd man out looking for grub and tables for groups. It's the restaurant at the end of the peninsula…at the Shangri-La Resort.

The relaxed vacation spot near Mount Ida is known as a good place for bargain stays on the lake. It's inexpensive, clean and down-home. At the diner, you can get yourself a good breakfast, burger or plate lunch—all while staring across the room at the daily selection of pies.

They come in all sorts of varieties—apple, peach, cherry and blueberry fruit pies; chocolate and coconut meringue; and whatever cream pies Varine Carr has come up with. Mrs. Carr, as they call her, has been making theses pies for decades—thirty a day, every day of the season, which runs from the first of February through the middle of November. Her salty-dough crust complements everything, and she makes it all from scratch—the meringue, sure, but also the chocolate and coconut custards, the icebox pies, the apple and peach and cherry fillings. All of them, from scratch.

Some swear by her chocolate pie, but I have to say it's the fruit pies I love the most, especially topped with an ample scoop of vanilla ice cream. They're all served warm unless you say you'd like it cool, which you're crazy if you do.

The Wagon Wheel Restaurant

You can't get more country diner than the square building alongside U.S. 65 south of Greenbrier. It's one of those places where local farmers and small business workers and owners meet over hamburger steak, ham or fried chicken for lunch. While the menu features sandwiches and burgers, there's always a large number of items on an old whiteboard meant to tempt the senses.

The Wagon Wheel Restaurant does all the things a good Arkansas country restaurant should do—serve fried catfish, respect and offer the different sorts of local side dishes available and show off the day's pie in a glass-front case. Out of all of those, the best are the meringue pies—particularly the extra-fine coconut meringue and the chocolate meringue. The custard is smooth, the crust is a little salty and the meringue has a great consistency.

Strawberry fried pie at Capital Bar and Grill at the Capital Hotel. *Kat Robinson*.

PART II

The Innovators and the Industrious

Pies made by some of the brightest, most energetic and most creative chefs in the state

Ashley's and Capital Bar and Grill at the Capital Hotel

Tandra Watkins can bake amazing croissants, cookies, bread, wedding cakes and more. But her pies come from the heart.

Tandra Watkins is a fireball. The talented pastry chef is in charge of things bready and sweet at the Capital Hotel in downtown Little Rock. She crafts fine and fancy desserts for Ashley's, the four-star restaurant and brightest diamond in the state's dining scene. She also creates the southern-inspired sweets served up at Capital Bar and Grill, the hotel's other restaurant and popular lunch spot for the white-collar crowd. Add in-suite service, private dining, banquets and the fabulous wedding cakes she fashions for the top tier of blissed newlyweds, and you can imagine she has a full dance card.

But she loves pie.

Her bio piece with the hotel talks about how she creates many of the delicacies she's become renowned for—but it ends with a quote from her very lips. "I adore pies," she says. "A good piece of pie is pure bliss—and I'll always have one on the menu."

Watkins was a military brat, raised by parents from Iowa who settled for some time in Cabot during her youth. She started in the restaurant business as a prep cook and did catering on the side. And then her husband's job took them to France. Not knowing a word of French and presented with a unique opportunity, she enrolled at Le Cordon Bleu and found her true calling as a pastry chef. When her husband's job moved the family again, she stayed on to finish her degree there.

Tandra Watkins, pastry chef at Ashley's and Capital Bar and Grill at the Capital Hotel in Little Rock. *Grav Weldon*.

When she returned to Arkansas, she reached out to Chef Lee Richardson, who had just signed on as executive chef at the Capital Hotel, which at the time was being remodeled. He took a liking to her and made her his pastry chef, and she suddenly found herself in the thick of a whole new world.

You know the saying "sink or swim"? There was plenty of potential for Watkins to sink in the turbulent waters of a legendary hotel that was opening with not one but two tremendous restaurants. Instead, she took the challenge happily. Word has spread around these parts about her incredible aptitude and general good humor.

I've been very fortunate to work with Watkins on all sorts of different projects. My life as a freelancer made it possible for me to have a thumb in every pie, as it were. One of those pie-like projects was working with a cherry distributor to find chefs to make an on-the-spot fantastic dish. Tandra's pistachio crème brulee with Rainier cherries and pistachio shortbread cookies was created within hours of the challenge, and it was marvelous. Another time when I was working with the inaugural Arkansas Cornbread Festival, she baked and served up a marvelously beautiful pan of corn bread that became the heart of our pre-event promotional photography. And, just to let you know, her chocolate croissants are ethereal.

Creating desserts for two completely different restaurants can be a challenge, and the crews in the kitchens at the Capital Hotel have an additional initiative to follow—to utilize local ingredients in the evolution and realization of every dish. So the desserts, just like every other dish, tend to be seasonal.

For Capital Bar and Grill, pies are a standard. Throughout the summer months, there's always a fried pie on the menu, and they change with the crops. They usually run strawberry, blueberry, peach and blackberry, and when the season is done they're gone too (though you'll see apple fried pies all through the year). The flaky-crusted fork-tined pies could come from any Delta kitchen, a crispy flour and butter pastry crust concealing fresh fruit spiced just so, served up with house-made buttermilk ice cream.

Sometimes there are tarts, and sometimes there are out-and-out pie slices. The chocolate tart often makes an appearance, creamy and striking. The base custard of bittersweet chocolate balances against the sweet cocoa-blended whipped cream piped on top and the slightly salty tart crust below.

And with autumn comes sweet potato pie, spiced delightfully, served up with equally spiced roasted pecans and bacon brittle ice cream, all of it made in-house and all magnificently warming and comforting with a cup of coffee and some brown sugar cubes.

Comfort food is easy enough for the working crowd, but what about a place like Ashley's? Even here, Watkins is on her game. A lot of it is presentation. A lot is skill. And some of it is just paying attention to what's going to go well together. She's good at that.

For instance, her buttermilk pie. It's simple, but it's not. It's not a huge dessert. The pie is tiny, a mere three-inch round sliced in half, but it has that beautiful creamy tart custard that any good buttermilk pie should have, a nicely caramelized top under a dusting of powdered sugar and a curl of spiced whipped cream.

It's paired with an even tarter duo—a twinned smear of lemon custard and a dollop of lemon sorbet. The sorbet actually reaches a level of tartness only achieved through the proper application of absolutely fresh lemon juice, a delicious palate cleanser. The custard cries out for that bit of pie to go along with it, a yin-yang of slightly tart to mostly tart, creamy and yet so diametrically

Buttermilk tart at Ashley's at the Capital Hotel. *Kat Robinson*.

Brown sugar pie at Ashley's. *Kat Robinson*.

opposed, and a drizzle of simple syrup alongside for the perfect final touch. Just one more way Watkins manages to bring the pedestrian pie to a new plateau.

And then there's the brown sugar pie with bourbon cream. It'd be easy to reserve this for the upscale crowd at Ashley's, but Watkins instead offers it to the businessmen and women dining at Capital Bar and Grill. She received this pie recipe from Chef Bill Smith of Crook's Corner in Chapel Hill, North Carolina; it is adapted from a recipe from Nancy McDermott (the pie maven of the South). Watkins tells me, "The brown sugar custard puts the 'goo' in good…once you try it, you'll never be able to live without it!"

Brown Sugar Pie

Yield: one 9-inch pie

1¼ cups all-purpose flour
½ cup cake flour
2 tablespoons powdered sugar
1½ teaspoons kosher salt
4 ounces Crisco shortening, cold
4 ounces unsalted butter, cold and cut into cubes
1 large egg
1 tablespoon white vinegar
4 ounces ice water

In a food processor, process all the dry ingredients to whisk them together. Then add the Crisco and butter and pulse the mixture together until the butter is in little pea-sized pieces. Add the egg, vinegar and some of the water and start the machine, and slowly add the rest of the water. Stop the machine as soon as the dough starts to come together into a ball.

Turn the dough out onto a floured work surface and shape it into a disk. Wrap the dough with plastic wrap and chill for at least 2 hours.

To prepare the pie shell, flour a work surface and roll the chilled dough out ¼-inch thick. Transfer the dough to a 9-inch pie pan and press the dough into the bottom and corners of the pie pan. Trim the excess dough that hangs over the edge of the pan, about ½ inch past the lip of the pan. Tuck the overhang of dough just inside the edge of the pan and crimp the dough to your liking.

Place the prepared pie shell in the freezer to set while you prepare the filling. Preheat the oven to 350° Fahrenheit (or 325° for convection).

Brown Sugar Custard

1 pound light brown sugar
4 large eggs
¼ cup whole milk
½ tablespoon pure vanilla extract
¼ teaspoon kosher salt
4 ounces unsalted butter, melted

In a food processor or a stand mixer fitted with a whisk attachment, blend together the light brown sugar, eggs, milk, vanilla and salt until completely blended and smooth. With the machine running, slowly stream in the melted butter until it is all mixed in well. Pour the custard into the prepared pie shell and bake at 350° Fahrenheit (325° for convection) for 30 to 40 minutes, or until the pie is puffed and golden brown, if shaken will jiggle a little bit but will not be liquid at all. Allow the pie to cool completely before cutting and serving with bourbon whipped cream.

The Boardwalk Café

Boardwalk Café's Arkansas black walnut pie is locally sourced, dark and divine.

Arkansas has some fine restaurants—some that fall into haute cuisine, some that dwell in the comfort food region, some that have specialties that rival those in large cities. Many have staples like farm-raised catfish, greens and fried pies. Some even dabble in new directions with the slow food movement, produce from local farms and organics.

A few years ago, Arkansas grew its first all-organic restaurant, not in the capital city of Little Rock or even in central Arkansas. It sprouted a short distance from the Buffalo National River's swath through the Ozark Mountain plateau, in a tiny town called Jasper.

The Boardwalk Café overlooks the Little Buffalo River, part of a block-long complex that includes the Arkansas House, a rather nifty bed-and-breakfast; a hair salon that specializes in pampering guests; and the only health food store in all of Newton County. Joseph and Janet Morgan started the café in 2006. They decided to do something difficult in what might seem a rather unlikely place—offering a completely organic menu in a town not easy to access by eighteen-wheeler. They reached out to area farmers and offered them a chance to sell their produce locally, where it could be enjoyed at the peak of freshness. Most of the meat and just about all the produce the Morgans serve comes from thirty-five area farmers. Much of the meat comes from Ratchford Farms, an organic operation near Marshall that specializes in beef, buffalo and elk. The Morgans also raise their own cattle

Black walnut pie at Boardwalk Café in Jasper. *Grav Weldon.*

and swine. Greens come year-round from producers that swap the seasons with traditional farming and greenhouses. Most of the spices used at the Boardwalk Café come from flower and herb beds on the property.

From the first time I noticed the café that had sprung up in the old Dairy Diner location along Scenic Highway 7, I'd make a point to drop in. No one ever made a fuss about me and my tiny little camera, and I didn't have to explain the weird corn syrup intolerance I was developing. Each time I have found a similar experience—a warm atmosphere, clean restrooms, lovely artwork from local artists available for purchase and unique items of culinary delight to savor.

The Morgans make everything from gumbo to steak and whatever they decide they're going to come up with on any particular day. But one thing that's always on the menu is the black walnut pie. It's a singular find in my travels—a pie made from the dark and almost pungent nuts of the black walnut tree. I've dropped in just for that pie—that burnished sweet warm treat that recalls cool autumn days in front of a stone hearth, shelling walnuts and thinking about Thanksgiving. There is something about the flavor of black walnuts that reminds me of childhood and fall, picking up the big round nuts out of the yard and watching an adult carefully but adeptly smack them with a hammer to get to the meat inside.

The sorghum molasses speaks to me from when I had it on biscuits with butter as a kid. Deep, dark tones that unapologetically claim they're the flavor of Arkansas bottomlands. I dig it. The pie is made with black and English walnuts, that sorghum molasses and cane syrup—no Karo Nut here. It's served with a scoop of black walnut ice cream, an extra emphasis I thoroughly enjoy.

The pie is five dollars a slice or twenty-four dollars for a whole pie, which may seem a little hefty for a small-town diner. But it is worth it. I do have to tell you, it's a cultured taste, a flavor that will smack you upside the head and remind you that you're in the Natural State.

The Greenhouse Grille

Greenhouse Grille's bourbon chocolate chunk pecan pie is irresistible.

When one goes about researching such a broad subject as pie and talks about it with others and chronicles the search with a blog and printed pieces and TV appearances, one is often asked a singular question: what's your favorite pie?

While it may be politically tumultuous to actually answer that question, I finally came to an answer. And that's not to say that there are no other good pie places in Arkansas—it's to say that this was the froth on top of the cream of the crop. It was my favorite of any pie I tried.

It's the bourbon chocolate chunk pecan pie from Greenhouse Grille in Fayetteville. I keep dreaming of it. I'm surprised I haven't accidentally eaten my pillow dreaming about it. It's that good.

Greenhouse Grille has been on my radar since it opened in Fayetteville in 2006. Today, the restaurant is set up next door to where the local farmers' market meets. From outside, the building beckons with planters and beds of herbs, vegetables and shrubs that are utilized by Chef Jerrmy Gawthrop throughout the menu. Inside, the restaurant sports a casual bar up front and a cavernous dining room beyond, with a small stage area, perfect for acoustic artists who perform at the restaurant on a regular basis.

Chef Gawthrop has also partnered the restaurant with dozens of local farmers and meat and dairy producers to create its menu. He brings in freshly made bread from Ozark Natural Breads and coffee from Arsaga Coffee Roasters. The

Bourbon chocolate chunk pecan pie at Greenhouse Grille in Fayetteville. *Grav Weldon.*

restaurant recycles its cooking oil for biodiesel, utilizes house-filtered local water for drinking and cooking and even composts its organic waste.

The food is inspired and tasty. I always have to order up some shiitake mushroom fries with "Magic Catsup." I love the parmesan risotto balls, the lamb and herb meatballs, the variations on the house burger and more. But the pie...well, I get the pie every single time I go.

You have to start off with the cookie-type crust. It's like a chocolate chip cookie, I kid you not. And then there are the chocolate chunks themselves—blueberry-sized chunks of goodness. The pecan custard is infused with more of that cookie flavor, and that bourbon flavor permeates the whole thing. The top is crisp like a brownie.

And it's always accompanied by a scoop of vanilla ice cream and some seasonal fruit—and that's where it really turns into something special. Take a bit of strawberry, a bit of the hot pie and a bit of the cool ice cream and place them all together on your tongue. Now sigh—because it is that good. The locally roasted house coffee is the perfect accompaniment, by the way, rich and velvety with lovely nutty notes.

They have the pie whenever Greenhouse Grille is open, whether it's lunch any day except Monday or dinner any day except Sunday or Monday—that is, unless they run out. And if they run out, I am so sorry. You're just going to have to make a return trip. You'll find Greenhouse Grille at 481 South School in Fayetteville.

Bourbon Chocolate Chunk Pecan Pie

(Makes 2 pies)

6 medium eggs

2 cups brown rice syrup (or corn syrup)

2 cups brown sugar

$^1/_3$ cup bourbon (Jack Daniels)

4 ounces semi-sweet chocolate chunks

2 pie crusts, blind-baked

$2^2/_3$ cups toasted pecans

Beat eggs until smooth. Slowly add syrup and brown sugar. Pour in bourbon and mix thoroughly.

Place chocolate chunks across bottom of pie shells. Pour batter over the chocolate. Top with pecans.

Place on sheet pan and bake in preheated 350° oven for 45 to 50 minutes or until center is firm.

Hunka Pie

Chris Monroe of Hunka Pie is either brilliant or crazy. Or both.

Traditionally, a restaurant might have three to five pies on its menu. If it's a bona fide pie shop, maybe there are a dozen. Can you imagine having your choice of one hundred different pies?

Can you imagine them being made by one person in one night?

Chris Monroe is a man with an obsession. That obsession is called Hunka Pie. Usually you'll find anywhere from five to eight different pies on the menu there. But a while back, Chris came up with an unusual idea: he decided to bake one hundred different varieties of pie in a single night for sale in a grand pie extravaganza the next day.

Thing is, Hunka Pie is a great place for a pie (and a burger, most days) to pick up and take with you. Today it's located in North Little Rock in an old Streamliner diner. But at the time, it was operating out of the former location of The Hop, a drive-in restaurant with no inside dining and almost no parking. Heck, there was barely enough room inside for Monroe and his help.

It didn't matter. One Saturday afternoon in August 2011, Monroe got to baking around 2:00 p.m. and wrapped up his quest around 3:00 a.m. on Sunday morning. He managed to make every pie on his list—except one. The lime margarita didn't come out. No matter, he made pineapple custard instead.

So how do you go about storing one hundred different pies (actually more, there were duplicates) in such a small space? You store them everywhere—

The line started early and swept far at Hunka Pie. *Kat Robinson.*

inside and on top of the pie case, on the cooled griddle-top, on every available counter and surface and even inside the drink cooler.

There were more than a dozen people lined up when I arrived that day, nearly fifteen minutes before the scheduled opening at noon, and Monroe had decided to go ahead and start doing business. Every parking spot was soon filled. He let me come behind the fence and into the tiny shop, as long as I stayed out of the way. That wasn't easy; there was barely enough room for the pie maker and two of his lackeys! With so many pies, I was shocked at how efficient they were—and that they knew where every pie happened to be located.

And what sort of pies? Among the many offerings were sweet potato, caramel apple, peach lattice, lemon icebox, peach blueberry, chocolate bananas foster, apple pear, coconut custard, sweet potato pecan, banana cream, chocolate chess, Butterfinger, cherry lattice, Key lime and egg custard. And that's just a start.

So many pies—and so many customers. Close to fifty had been through by the time I got to the front counter with my list. Pie slices were $3.50 each, with a six-pack going for $20.00. The variety was extraordinary. I picked up a slice of the shop's favorite, the Velvet Lips chocolate cream, and one of

Pies covered every surface, including the stove top, at Hunka Pie. *Kat Robinson*.

my favorites, the pear ginger pie. The other four I'd never tried before: sugar (like a fluffy sugar cookie), pumpkin cream cheese, macadamia nut (like a pecan pie but with macadamias instead) and cherry chipotle. This last one has to be the strangest cherry pie I have ever sampled—an almost savory cherry pie with deep peppery but only mildly spicy notes.

The event was scheduled to run from noon until 6:00 p.m., but by 4:00 p.m. the event was about six slices from completely selling out.

Will Monroe try it again? He says he's thinking about it. The day of the event, he seemed like he was going to fall down. But Monroe is a showman, and I would suspect that he'll try an even bigger feat the next time around.

302 on the Square

Architecture, food and a hootenanny every Friday night—Berryville's 302 on the Square is far more than just a restaurant.

Ever just have a dream you want to follow? Ever been brave enough to follow that dream? Alexander Virden has been following dreams for a while. His latest dream could change the face of downtown Berryville.

Virden used to work on oil rigs off the Louisiana coast. He lived in Algier's Point, just a ferry ride from New Orleans's French Quarter. Injuries forced him to leave his job as a diver, but he continued on by working to restore homes here and there.

Virden did eventually leave Louisiana, setting off in an RV and just driving where he felt. Something made him stop at Berryville, and that's where his roaming ceased.

"I asked about this building," he told me one Saturday afternoon during a late lunch. "I asked about this big building, and no one could remember what it was. I said, 'You know that building between that little shop and the post office?' And people had just ignored it."

That building was the old Grand View Hotel. It started off life auspiciously as the Saint George Hotel back in 1902 with a gala dance in its grand ballroom. But the property passed through a number of hands in its first decade. M.M. Hoagland added the balconies and porches to it shortly after he took it over in 1910. Mr. and Mrs. L.C. Smith bought the place in 1926 and renamed it the Grand View Hotel.

302 on the Square in Berryville. *Grav Weldon*.

Dr. John H. Bohannan bought the hotel in 1943. He eventually added the commercial spaces in front of the hotel for more revenue. But by the early 1970s, the hotel was closed. It was purchased in 1984 by Phillis and Carl Loehr, who attempted a massive reconstruction of the building but were unable to finish. It sat fallow for the better part of two decades, gathering bird droppings and an amazing amount of stored-away junk. "You couldn't walk straight through anywhere," Virden told me. "You'd have to turn sideways. To get through this dining room there was a path from here to the hall. There was scaffolding, there was stuff packed all the way up to the scaffolding and then stuff on top of it. On the stairs it was packed so tight you only had a path just wide enough to go up or down. We hauled out more than 250 cubic yards of junk."

"We" in this case would be Virden and his partner, Sandra Doss. While we were there for lunch, we heard muted noises from the kitchen where she was working. I got the impression she was rather shy.

Virden's dream when he saw the hotel was to refurbish it—not just as a potential hotel but as an art space. He wants to encourage the arts in the small town. He also runs Ozarts.org and is working hard with the Ozark Animation Club, a grass-roots effort to create a school for students of 3D animation.

The hotel, though, had so many possibilities. There are fourteen rooms with en-suite baths above the first floor, still in the renovation process but so much further along than they were when Virden first bought the place in November 2005. On the fourth floor there's a grand open space Virden hopes to utilize as event space—a large area with its own kitchen that might host artists' receptions, weddings and the like. The rooms could be let to artists in residence, possibly. Possibilities seem to be the order of the day.

But the main focus these past three years has been on the restaurant. 302 on the Square is part of Virden's dream—not just as part of his hotel complex but to finance the completion of the renovations. It's a time-consuming effort, running an eatery—and it's eaten into time for actually working on the hotel. But it's also a labor of love.

The recipes at 302 on the Square are family recipes. The restaurant itself is billed as a "Cajun-American" eatery. "We do the American favorites, hamburger and hot dogs," Virden says. "And we do the kind of food I know from Louisiana, the red beans and rice and stuff."

I have been taken by a singular dish, the South Carolina strawberries and cream, only available when strawberries are in season. The marinated berries and heavy cream are served up over a hot flaky biscuit rather than the expected shortcake. The saltiness of that biscuit balances perfectly with the sweetness of the cream and the tartness of the berries.

And then there's something the restaurant serves that I can only describe as a memento of my childhood. The dish, listed on the menu as Louisiana Chicken and Gravy, is straight out of my grandmother's recipe book. The thick skillet pepper gravy, smothered free-range chicken (all the restaurant's poultry comes from Little Portion Monastery), that flavor of homemade poultry seasoning and a little thyme and butter, all served over a mound of extra-long grain rice, is the sort of thing that will take me back. It's warm and hearty and peppery and…I lose myself in the dish.

Catfish, corn bread, a Reuben sandwich—it's all there, all these southern favorites that so well represent the rural culture of Louisiana, Arkansas and the mid-South. Down to hush puppies and green tomato relish, too. Doss has managed to make a worthy coleslaw as well. "She makes it all up in small batches," Virden told me. "She cuts up the cabbage and stuff and makes up the dressing separately, and she only combines them a little bit at a time as we go along." It works. The crunchy vegetation is matched with a sweet and creamy dressing that doesn't have any hint of staleness to it.

This is a long way to go without talking about pie, and the 302 has a doozy. Virden told me the recipe for his Dang Good Pie comes from a friend whose grandmother's grandmother had it in her collection. Five generations back, a recipe dating back to the nineteenth century—well now. We're talking about a pineapple-coconut pie.

My first thought when I tasted it was how buttery it was. It was very much like pineapple upside-down cake, but with coconut. It was almost meaty in texture, with such a strong and delicious brown sugar flavor to it. The crust was handmade too, unsweetened butter crust nice and crisp, with a little dotting of whipped cream to top it off.

Oh, if it were only about a pie. But pie doesn't pay the bills all by itself, and there's far more work to be done on the hotel. Virden's next project is to complete the renovation of the Garden Room on the back of the first level and to add a small greenhouse off the back so he and Doss can start growing their own herbs and vegetables to use in the restaurant. That's going to be quite a bit of work, but I'm sure they'll manage.

Oh, I did mention a hootenanny, didn't I? Virden's love for art continues every Friday night with local artists invited to come play in the dining room. Every week, musicians come in and jam the way the hollows around these parts have been jammed for more than a century—with good local folk music played on local instruments. It's an experience to hear the hoot and holler and kick back with a sing-along or two.

You'll find 302 on the Square on…well, the Berryville Square. East or west, you'll get there on U.S. 62. It's on the northeast corner—look for the tall building with the green awning.

Terry's Finer Restaurant

Even pie can be translated to elegant and upscale. Take, for instance, the apple tartine at Terry's Finer Restaurant in the Heights section of Little Rock. Known for its light French cuisine, Terry's has been a break-out in a food-loving city. Trey Adams has married the traditional Arkansas favorite of apple pie with the tenets of fine French cooking. The tartine is simple: Granny Smith apple slices, decadent spices, sugar and a blind-baked flat crust.

Apple tartine at Terry's Finer Restaurant in Little Rock. *Kat Robinson.*

Everything is beautifully caramelized, almost to the softball candy stage. How, though? Well, unlike most of the pies in this book, this one's baked upside down in a short-edge cast-iron skillet. It's served with light, unsweetened whipped cream on the side. And it is the perfect dish to complete a light summer lunch.

E's Bistro

Ever go to one place to try one thing and end up falling in love with something completely different? It happened to me at a tearoom-style lunch place called E's Bistro in North Little Rock. I went in to try a lemon hazelnut pie and ended up falling in love with something else.

That something else is the remarkable Hershey pie. It's a pretty pie, delivered topped with syrup and pecans, with a mint sprig and a pile of strawberries on the side. All the accoutrements, though, are unnecessary, since the pie itself is marvelous. The signature Hershey chocolate flavor is perfectly suspended in an impossibly light confection of cream just sweet enough to satisfy. I was expecting a heavy pie but got light and tasty, with just the right amount of salt and sugar in it to hit the right buttons.

So I wrote about my experience with the pie on the "Eat Arkansas" blog for the *Arkansas Times*. It wasn't an hour after the blog posted that I received a message from Elizabeth McMullen, the fascinating woman behind E's Bistro. She started out with Catering to Your Cravings in 1996. She's had clients ranging from Neil Diamond to Bob Villa of *This Old House* fame all the way up to President Bill Clinton. She had another restaurant called Elizabeth's on Crestwood for a while. And then there was E's.

She was insistent I come back, so I did, and I got to try not the lemon hazelnut pie I originally sought but a lemon pecan pie, and…well, have you ever had a life-changing pie? I'd never have considered making a pecan pie with a lemon custard, but Elizabeth did and it's marvelous. I was expecting something in one of two directions—either a lemon cream pie dotted with nuts or a pecan pie with some heavy bright yellow lemon custard within. I encountered neither of these. Instead, I found the pie enigmatic above its salty pastry crust. The lemon custard within was like a light version of a pecan pie custard yet lighter and less sweet, far less cloying, almost delicate. Above it hovered a layer of lemon-glazed pecans that acted more as a nutty, savory crust than a heavy player in the production.

Turns out she got the recipe from a customer. Well, I think that went well. Ask for it when you go, or call in advance to make sure it's there. Heck, I bet Elizabeth could make any pie fabulous.

Meringue pies at Charlotte's Eats and Sweets in Keo. *Kat Robinson*.

PART III

The Pie Powerhouses

You want pie? These are the places you can have pie with your pie, with a side order of pie.

Charlotte's Eats and Sweets

Charlotte's Eats and Sweets is nationally known—for good reason.

Five days a week at 11:00 a.m. in the miniscule Pulaski County burg of Keo, there's a line a block long of hungry people patiently waiting outside a single-story building off U.S. 165. They wait patiently, whether it's cold or hot, for a chance to share a table inside the hottest—indeed, the only—sit-down restaurant in town.

They're not locals. The locals know to call in their orders and pick them up. No, they call from all over the United States and elsewhere, for the opportunity to have a Keo Klassic sandwich and what *Southern Living* calls the best coconut meringue pie in the South.

But Charlotte's Eats and Sweets wasn't supposed to be about pie. It was a short-term situation Charlotte Bowls got herself into back in 1993. The building, which used to house a pharmacy, was still full of the furniture and stuff the previous owner had left behind more than a decade before. There wasn't much room, and she had to do a lot of clearing out before getting enough space for a tiny kitchen and counter together.

The folks in Keo were grateful for a good spot to grab a bite to eat, and they encouraged Charlotte to expand her menu. She worked, too, on clearing out the pharmacy front to back and utilizing every bit of room in the building. And as she cleared it out, the crowd just continued to fill every seat, day after day.

A lot of people have written about the pies at Charlotte's. It came my turn to do so back in the summer of 2010. I went early—too early, in fact. I got

Charlotte Bowls dollops meringue onto chocolate pies at Charlotte's Eats and Sweets. *Kat Robinson*.

there about a quarter after 10:00 a.m. on a Tuesday. I parked down the block and caught up on e-mail from my laptop while I waited. I'd been there a little while when I noticed motion to my right. I looked up and noticed about a half dozen people waiting outside. It was 10:39 a.m.

I kept watching for a bit as more people arrived. A minute before 11:00, a couple of big vans pulled up. I realized my discretion at having parked so far away may have been ludicrous, so I went ahead and headed in.

Inside, I glanced toward the back room; a few tables were already full, and the ones that weren't had place cards reserving them for large parties. I quickly dashed back to the last remaining empty two-top up front and planted myself there. It was 11:04.

The interior was comfortable, an old-style storefront, one of the last remaining on the stretch of street bypassed by the highway some years back. Giant glass-front cabinets occupied two whole walls of the front room, and a significant bar back with mirror graced the third, standing tall behind an old walnut soda fountain. The tables were wooden-topped cast-iron affairs, and they were all dotted with hungry folks eyeballing the pie list. The cases held items for sale, like jams and home crafts and figurines.

My waitress flitted by like the breeze, taking orders from a nearby table of seven before sweeping over and delivering a menu to me. "I'm so sorry," she apologized almost breathlessly. "Do you need a minute?"

"Yes, ma'am."

"Need a drink?"

"Iced tea."

"Sweet or un, hon?"

"Un, no lemon."

She smiled and moved on to the next table, handing out menus to the three ladies there and soaking up drink orders. Then she disappeared into a prep area out of view.

The rattle of conversation increased. No one seemed upset about the pace or the fact that it was quite packed inside. It was now 11:20 a.m., and no one in the front room had received any sort of sustenance. But no one complained. That, to me, said a lot about the place.

Not that there weren't people who gave up. I saw twice where groups of four to six came in, took one look and left. Their loss. There were a dozen people waiting in the front of the restaurant, and it looked like there were a good number of people outside, too.

My waitress returned with her notepad. "Have you decided?"

"The Keo Klassic. Oh, and could you describe your caramel pie?"

"It's a burnt sugar custard under meringue. I like it."

"I'll have that too."

She grinned and turned to the next table to pick up its order. The pie had been a hard choice. While the coconut pie at Charlotte's is highly recognized, the chocolate is also well known. The whiteboard also had egg custard and caramel written on it, and while I loved egg custard, I hadn't had a caramel before. I wondered if it'd be like butterscotch. I promised myself if I managed to make it through the repast I'd already ordered that I'd ask for a piece of egg custard, too.

My eyes were drawn to the delivery of a chocolate milkshake to the group table across the way. The tall glass screamed of dairy delights. It was the first dessert I had seen pass that morning, and it made my stomach rumble. Most of the tables were packed with people nursing beverages, and none of the tables had real food yet. But that was fine, since most of the tables were abuzz with conversation.

It'd taken fifteen to twenty minutes just to get that drink order, and here it was 11:30 a.m. and I was really starting to feel hungry. I heard the hostess, Kimberly, taking orders over the phone. There seemed to be just as many call-in orders as eat-in ones, and I couldn't imagine just how busy that kitchen must have been.

I just marveled—all those people waiting, all the ones already seated wanting food, what kept them there? Was the reputation of the place really that good, or was it the food? For heaven's sake, it was a Tuesday morning— not necessarily the busiest time of the week, eh?

Kimberly came over and bussed the table next to mine as she took an order on the phone. My eyes wandered back over to the specials board, which was advertising a fresh fruit plate with watermelon, strawberries, grapes, pineapple, bananas, cantaloupe and poppy seed dressing with a choice of chicken salad, tuna salad or cottage cheese and garlic biscuits to boot for $8.25. I was starting to see this special speed by me on its way to other tables.

All at once, two of the waitresses swept into the room with meals for the group of seven on the other side of the front room. Grilled ham and cheese sandwiches, round burgers and clubs were doled out, each with their cursory stack of rippled potato chips and a hearty slice of pickle.

The line had been constant, staying at even numbers despite the small influx of people as tables became available. At 11:40 a.m., few had received their meals, but still there was no complaint. I heard my waitress tell newcomers at another table, "Cobbler is Thursday, remember?" and give her wan smile again. I noticed she was taking dessert reservations with each dinner order. Apparently there is some small fear that a particular type of pie might run out before the customers get the chance to order.

In the back, it was a different story, where the big tables reserved early on were being served. The noise level never dipped, conversations continuing in between bites of sandwiches and salads and, of course, the inevitable pie.

There was a plunk on the table, and I looked up from my notepad where I had been quickly scribbling notes to catch a glimpse of my waitress and her earnest smile. "Your sandwich will be ready in a minute, hon," she beamed at me, refilling my tea. I smiled back and picked up my camera.

As I snapped away at the pie that had just been delivered to me, I overheard one of the ladies at the next table mutter, "It'd taste better if she ate it." I smiled in their direction, and they nodded back. It was hard to shoot with that decadent layer of meringue all full of bubbles and the custard. I shot it, but I couldn't wait for the rest of my lunch. One bite, and I knew I'd chosen well. That lovely burnt sugar taste of the custard, a caramel made from scratch and not some melted lump of stuff from Kraft, a gorgeous taste that could make you cry. The meringue, firm and yet able to grasp the custard well, was toasted on top, almost burnt but not quite, attaining a burnt sugar essence in its flavor. All of this sat on top of a lovely hand-thrown butter crust that mated well to the whole pie. I could not help myself. I had to dig in.

Mere moments later, my plate arrived, and I looked up at the waitress guiltily. She just smiled. I'm sure I'm not the first person who's passed through the doors at Charlotte's and eaten dessert first.

Well, I had to work, you know. This was, after all, what I did. I put down my fork and started shooting the sandwich under its cover of rippled potato chips. The Keo Klassic's nice crust made by the parmesan garlic batter on the grill was crispy, while the bread underneath was still white and fluffy. The thin layers below spoke of tastiness—Monterey Jack cheese, smoked turkey breast, tomato, white onion, avocado and another slice of Monterey Jack. It was all somehow smooth and juicy at the same time, holding together with each bite. It was soft in the middle and warm, like this incredible interpretation marrying grilled cheese and a fresh turkey sandwich. I adored it.

I was halfway through the first half of the sandwich and watching the line up front. One of the waitresses announced, "Be sure when you get through the door you get your name on the waiting list." You wouldn't think of reservations for a down-home establishment like Charlotte's, but it really is that popular. I heard my waitress tell the table next to mine that a church group of twenty-two had come in and stalled up the orders a bit. The ladies at that table waved her off, not concerned about the time it had taken to receive their order. Time's not a big issue for most diners here, I came to find.

I was about halfway through the sandwich when the waitress came to my table. "Can I get you anything else?" she asked as she freshened my tea.

"Egg custard, please. To go."

"You got it!" she beamed. She pulled out my check, marked it and flipped it onto the table. I finished my sandwich and returned my attention to the pie, which had been calling my name throughout the meal. It was just as good if not better.

I heard another waitress call for a party of eight to follow her to the back about the time my egg custard arrived in its little clamshell box. I couldn't help but photograph it right then and there. Then I took one more swig of my tea and hopped up to get in line to pay. There were, after all, people waiting. My table was bussed and ready to go before I even got to the head of the line. Paid up, a couple of bucks handed off to the ladies at the next table to hand to my waitress when she came back around again and I was out the door. Another dozen people were standing around and sitting on provided benches, calmly waiting their turn despite the ninety-something-degree heat.

It's amazing to me that such a humble place receives that sort of attention. I should have expected it—after all, when I mentioned on Facebook that I was in Keo, there was a collective swoon of pie lovers. But nothing prepared me for the volume of people I would see pass through those doors.

Mama Max's Diner

Mama Max's serves up home-grown and home-cooked favorites with a side of pie.

I love home cooking. I really can't get enough of it. I don't mean greasy home fries and some thrown-together stuff that some restaurants call home cooking. I'm talking about the sort of food your mamma would cook for ya if she had the time and really loved you. The sort of food I can recall from childhood, everyday stuff we'd have whenever, usually heavy on vegetables and light on meat.

I done had a meal like that at Mama Max's in Prescott—and the best part was, I also got a great dessert. Can't beat that with a stick.

The sign on the restaurant proclaims the place Maxine's Diner (Mama Max's is written on the window), and the little flat building is the dominion of Maxine Milner. Her children and grandchildren all work in the restaurant and have for the past twenty years. Maxine's an old-fashioned cook. Everything she makes, she makes from scratch, whether it's the hand-pulled and washed turnip greens or the hand-cut and seasoned creamed corn. And especially the pies.

There's a pie case when you walk in that, depending on the time of day and the day of the week, will be anywhere from half to completely full of pies and cakes and whatnot. Pies are $3.00 a slice, cakes $2.50 and the homemade turtles $2.00. The lemon icebox pie is homogenously smooth and sweet with just the right amount of tartness.

The real star I found in Mama's pie case, though, was the caramel apple nut pie, a prime southern pie filled with heat-softened chunks of pecans in

Mama Max's Diner in Prescott.
Grav Weldon.

Caramel apple pie at Mama Max's. *Kat Robinson.*

between two different types of slow-cooked apples. The crust was nice and savory, a salted top and bottom flaky crust that soaked up the apple essence quite well. What made it so good, though, was the drizzle of melted caramel over the top. That burnt sugar flavor was just the right thing to balance the tart apples and meaty pecans. That dang pie ate like a meal, and I was already about stuffed. But I ate it. I ate it all, even though it hurt. It was too good to leave.

You'll find Mama Max's at 1102 West Main Street in Prescott—that's Highway 24. If you take the first Prescott exit from I-40 heading south (the one with the Low's Truck Stop), it's a short jaunt down on the left.

Red Rooster Bistro

Endless pie at the Red Rooster Bistro in Alma

Years ago, Alma was the place to stop for good pie. Travelers would stop in off Interstate 40 and have a bite at the old Red Rooster Inn on U.S. 71. It was of legend. A couple years back, the place shut down. Suddenly, Alma's best claim to pie fame was gone. Sure, you still went to Alma to celebrate spinach and to see the Popeye statue, but that was about it.

(I kid, my Alma friends. Alma's a great little city. Alma High School, home of the Airedales—I kid you not—would always whup up on the Vilonia Eagles. My brother Zack played football for Vilonia. Don't get him started.)

Anyway, where was I? Well, one of the first things I discovered on my pie search was that this place some called the best in the Arkansas River Valley had closed, and I was just out of luck. Not long after I began my research, requests came in for me to go to Alma to check out a place. I just assumed it was this dead restaurant.

Then my photographer showed up at my door one day with a couple of those little white Styrofoam boxes that I was going to become oh so familiar with. And one of them contained a banana cream pie with nuts on it. Crazy. But it was pretty good. Turns out he got it at the Kountry Xpress, a truck stop off the Dyer exit along I-40. That's cool.

Next time down, he brought a piece of Tollhouse pie for our group to taste. It was like eating a big light cookie—not too heavy, not too rich,

Toll House pie at Red Rooster Bistro in Alma. *Grav Weldon.*

kinda crumbly and generally well liked. I thought that was a winner. It tasted, I kid you not, like the absolute best and thickest chocolate chip cookie I'd ever had.

And then there was the strawberry pie. When I tried it, I thought I was going to cry. It tasted like the absolute best strawberry pie I'd ever had at that point, down at Strawn's Eat Shop in Shreveport. It was that good—not too gelatinous, nicely tart and sweet. And then there was the sundae pie—a banana cream pie with a delightful layer of pineapple foam between top and bottom, drizzled in chocolate syrup with maraschino cherries on top.

And the Butterfinger pie—by that point, everyone was bringing pie to my house as they learned about my quest, and this one was so good I ate it out of the box with my bare fingers. My my.

I learned that there was a woman making these pies by the name of Brenda Gregory. She owned the Kountry Xpress, but she was also making pies for a place called the Red Rooster Bistro. It was time for me to go get some pie. I arranged a break in my schedule for the drive to Alma.

My dining companion and I went to the Red Rooster for dinner one afternoon, and the first thing I noticed was this big chalkboard on the left-hand wall. It went floor to ceiling and listed nearly thirty different types of desserts—most of them pies. We're talking apple, buttermilk, cherry, chocolate, coconut, egg custard, Hershey, lemon icebox, millionaire, peanut butter, Reese's, strawberry cream cheese, strawberry crepe, chocolate peanut butter, Butterfinger, banana split, creamy banana pecan, Key lime, German chocolate, lemon meringue, pecan, pecan cream cheese, strawberry, Tollhouse and peach cobbler. It was overwhelming. There was a checkmark beside about one-third of the names, and it turned out those were the pies they had on hand at the time.

We ordered our sandwiches (he the Airedale, I the Dagwood) and our slices of pie at the same time, on the recommendation of the waitress. Seems they make a certain number of pies each day, and once one is gone, it's gone. The sandwiches were massive and served on bread made right there at the restaurant, a cross between sourdough and King's Hawaiian Bread. We tried the fries and the beans and corn bread, all of which were excellent.

The German chocolate pie my companion ordered was amazing—a great brownie-type pie laced through with coconut and bits of pecans, not too sweet and very dense. It was quite spectacular.

But it paled in comparison to the star attraction at Red Rooster Bistro—its pecan cream cheese pie. How to describe this? It's a standard cream cheese base, slightly but not too strongly sweetened, topped with drippy pecans in their own sticky syrup, like the topping you'd get on a sticky bun. Layered atop a simple flour-butter blind-baked crust, that syrup permeates the cream cheese just enough to adhere the cream cheese filling to both top and bottom. Delightful.

I quickly learned the secret of obtaining Ms. Gregory's pie. If it was late and the restaurant was close to closing, I bypassed it altogether and went down to the Kountry Xpress and picked a piece of pie out of the case down there. That's how I discovered the marvelous peach cream cheese pie in 2011. I happened to be coming through the area right when peaches were in season. I was told peach season is the only time of year the pie is made, and it was wonderful. The peaches were still a tiny bit crunchy, and the center pinked the cream cheese just so.

For whatever reason—maybe the restaurant was doing really well, who knows?—Ms. Gregory sold the Kountry Xpress. I knew it within a week or two of the sale because I stopped in and there were no pies! That was all right, though. When I got up the road to Alma, the pie case at the Red Rooster was packed, and there were new flavors inside, like Amish peanut butter pie and a toffee pie. Wow. So head your way up to Alma and enjoy the handiwork of Brenda Gregory.

Bobby's Country Cookin'

Bobby's Country Cookin' offers meat, two veg and a case of pie delights.

Every weekday, there's a line that starts to form right before 11:00 a.m. outside a lunchroom off Shackleford Road in Little Rock. If you get there by that time, chances are you can be in and seated within fifteen minutes, no problem. If you get there at noon, forget about it. Lunch is going to take you more than an hour, and you're going to put up with it too—because you're dining at Bobby's.

The restaurant, Bobby's Country Cookin', started up years ago over on Sixty-fifth Street. It moved to West Little Rock in the aughts, and its popularity has never waned. It is still, to this day, the place to get home cooking for lunch on the new side of the city.

The line never ebbs between 11:00 a.m. and about 1:30 p.m. The menu is posted on the wall (and online too, once a week) and features good things to eat, like Mexican chicken casserole, spaghetti with meat sauce, steamed cabbage and Great Northern beans and stewed tomatoes, and always fried catfish on Fridays. It's a meat-and-two-veg sort of place.

What's not included in the package price are the pies, made from scratch each and every morning. Some pies never change—there's always coconut and chocolate pies, pecan pie and cherry cream cheese pie. Every single day. And every day has a different extra pie, like Key lime or vanilla chocolate chip or lemon icebox, mint chocolate chip or

Pies at Bobby's Country Cookin' in Little Rock. *Kat Robinson.*

peanut butter or strawberry. They're not fancy, but they're always exactly what you'd expect to have if someone was making you a pie at home. That's especially comforting.

Jenny Lind Country Café

Off the highway a bit, Bob and Wanda's Jenny Lind Country Café offers nostalgia and a whole case of sweet goodness.

By this point in the book, you've probably figured out that pie is everywhere in Arkansas. There's something quintessentially Arkansas about pie in all its various incarnations. A restaurant that doesn't serve pie (outside of the odd ethnic joint) is just not part of the Arkansas landscape.

The variants of pie go from the humble fried pie to the glory of a cream cheese sweet, from custard to cream to fruit to nut. Whether topped by meringue, nuts, whipped topping or a pastry lid, you're bound to find it at an Arkansas eatery. The pie culture permeates our state identity, just as surely as you'll find a Reuben sandwich on any menu around these parts.

Because we as customers subject ourselves to so many variants of pie, we become connoisseurs, which drives us to places like DeValls Bluff for Ms. Lena's Pies, to Ed and Kay's in Benton for their Mile-High pie and to Charlotte's Eats and Sweets in Keo. The names are all familiar, and we beat down the reeds on these paths to get where the pie is good.

The bar has been set high. For anything exceptional to break through, it has to be out-of-this-world good.

As you can guess, my pie obsession has led me down many roads, and I follow the recommendations of others down back roads and to little burgs here and there. So it wasn't unusual for me to follow a lead from photographer Grav Weldon to check out a little joint in the community of

Bob and Wanda's Jenny Lind Country Café near Greenwood. *Grav Weldon.*

Old Jenny Lind back in the summer of 2010. It took a little looking, but we finally found our way down Gate 9 Road to the Jenny Lind Country Café.

Inside and out, Americana clings to the place. A piano greets you when you come in the door. The waitresses are friendly, and the tables are comfortable. There are signs on the wall and sneakers hanging from the ceiling. The chairs and tables don't match, but that's all part of the charm.

We started out with a quick bit of disappointment. The pie we'd come seeking—the Chocolate Joy—was gone for the day. So were many of the other options. We stood at the pie case and whimpered a little, trying to gather up the gumption to try something else.

I figured out my choice of poison first: the buttermilk pie. Grav dithered over whether or not to do the chocolate until the lady behind the counter revealed that the Butterfinger crunch pie was still available. Well, there you go. We had our two selections.

Now, in case it hasn't become apparent, you should know that I will shoot anything that doesn't move (and a few things that do) in my efforts to bring you the essence of my food experience. Multiply by two, with

The pie case at Bob and Wanda's Jenny Lind Country Café. *Grav Weldon*.

Grav shooting as well, and you not only get a lot of photographs but you also collect odd looks from the clientele and questions from the staff. Lots of questions. Did this perturb us? Nah. Between the two of us, I think we took close to two thousand shots that particular day (of course, I am exaggerating a little). That's just what you do when you're trying to capture the goodness that is pie.

And that's the thing. These weren't average pies. It was revealed to us that pie baking began at six o'clock in the morning, and once the baking was done that was it—when the slices of a certain pie run out, they're gone. Though we missed out on the Chocolate Joy, we each found a bit of something salivating in our selections. The Butterfinger Crunch pie was far lighter than I had anticipated, a creamy refrigerated pie with just a little crunch to it in forms of tiny sparks of the named candy bar. Unlike other examples I'd had in this particular category, it wasn't overpowering, just sweet enough and with a crust that tasted like bits of the Butterfinger had been folded into the butter and flour of the pastry.

My choice, the buttermilk pie, was a new take on the old favorite. Most of the examples of buttermilk pie I've experienced have been in the chess pie range—custardy with a bubbly toasted top, usually on a rolled pastry bottom but every once in a while poured over a loose graham bottom. This one was quite different. The largest difference was the prominence of coconut. The flavor was complementary and so mildly sweet as to be comforting. The crust had become a little cakey; whether this was to do with the actual baking or the fact that we'd arrived at the little café twelve hours after it had been set to bake, I couldn't tell you. But it was pleasing, a real black-cup-of-coffee companion with its sweetly toasted top and substantial consistency.

Yes, indeed, we did drive quite a way just for pie. It was worth it.

Since my initial visit, I have been back many times, and in June 2012, the place changed hands. Today, it's Bob and Wanda's Jenny Lind Country Café, but the pies are still being made by the same woman who made them before, and they're still just as good. My only concern is that by letting out this secret, too many people might show up to eat pie before I can return any particular day. Well, that's the thing: you gotta take that chance.

Miss Anna's on Towson

Miss Anna's on Towson is still charming the sweet tooth of a community.

A generation of Fort Smith diners enjoyed home-grown dinners and great pies at Goodson's at Cornerstone. Starting in 1986, the restaurant served up Kickin' Chicken, pot roast burgers and other comfort foods six nights a week, along with some fantastic pies. A second location, Goodson's on Towson, was opened and found equally as worthy.

But in 2011, the restaurant scene on the Western Wall was in an uproar, and for some crazy reason the Goodson folks decided they wanted to do something different. After twenty-five years, they sold off both restaurants and opened Goody's, a yogurt shop, which honestly flummoxed a whole lot of people. Fortunately, someone stepped in. Or some place. The folks that run Ed Walker's up the road from the Towson location bought it, borrowed some pies and both places have done well for it. And thus was born Miss Anna's on Towson.

It's a lunchroom, yes. There are bits of memorabilia on the walls inside, though the exterior is not much to look at. And when you walk in, your eye is instantly drawn to a massive case full of pies. Well, pies and cakes and other desserts, but mostly pies, a dozen or more at a time. And it's one of those places where if you hit it in the right season, you can get decadent fresh fruit delights like peach cream cheese pie, blueberry pie and blackberry pie and even a home-style fresh apple pie. They also do a fantastic chocolate peanut butter pie, coconut meringue and more. It's hard to choose the best.

Cherry crisp at Miss Anna's on Towson in Fort Smith. *Grav Weldon.*

But I can slim it down to two you have to try. One of them is the chocolate pie, alternately called Chocolate Heaven or Chocolate Pile or whatever anyone else decides to name it. This thing is chocolate. It starts from the bottom crust—not a graham cracker crust, not an Oreo crust but, I kid you not, a chocolate chip cookie crust. The custard is rich and slightly bittersweet. There are chocolate chips and flakes throughout. The cream on top is also flaked with chocolate, and there's a chocolate Hershey's Kiss on each slice. It's chocolate and chocolate and chocolate, and just about anywhere else, it'd be the hands-down choice.

But then there's the cherry crisp. It's overwhelmingly good, not just with the deliciously rich but not too sweet cream filling but with the hand-pressed homemade pecan sandy crust. The blind-baked pecan and flour crust is crisp, and the nuttiness offers great contrast to the impossibly smooth custard. The tart gelatinous cherry topping plays perfectly with everything else.

You want to visit? If you're not familiar with the town and are coming in from elsewhere, the best way to get there is to take I-540 to Zero Street, go west and then go with the curve when it curves onto Towson. It's a few blocks down on the right.

Hillbilly Hideout

Hillbilly Hideout at the I-40 Travel Center serves up some of the best in Arkansas pie.

I tend to like truck stops. They usually offer decently clean bathrooms, twenty-four-hour service and some crazy items. And sometimes they have good restaurants, though that tends to be the older places.

This place I'm going to tell you about opened at the end of May 2012, but it has the flavor of a well-established restaurant. It's the I-40 Travel Center in Ozark—more so, it's Hillbilly Hideout, the restaurant inside. It could be the next great Arkansas gem in the making.

I stopped by briefly on my way to the Wakarusa Music Festival the weekend the place opened, and it was packed. Mind you, that's saying something, since a couple of football fields' worth of concrete was laid down for all the expected traffic to the place. I managed to get some iced tea and noticed there were fried pies by the register, and I made a mental note to head back over that way.

Well when I went up to the Altus Grape Festival a couple months later, I decided to stop in. There were a lot of people there, but nowhere near what I had experienced before. I had my daughter Hunter along for the ride. Now, I should let you know, I was hot and exhausted, and so was she. After we had spent a good portion of the day at the Grape Festival, we had checked out the Backwoods Arts Gathering up at Mulberry Mountain—and saw the effect the one-hundred-plus-degree heat had on that event. We wanted a good meal, a cool place to sit and plenty of iced tea to soak in.

First thing I noticed when we went in is that there's this deli bar at the end of the restaurant. At the deli bar, you can get just about everything you'd ever expect from a truck stop—taquitos, jojo potatoes, pizza sticks, hot dogs, chicken fingers, cold sandwiches, fried chicken, fried shrimp, chicken on a stick, frog legs, hush puppies, catfish, ribs and beef brisket. So it was like a deli, a truck stop warming box and a BBQ joint all rolled into one.

And right by the register were these big eight-inch-long fried pies. And they were tempting. But as I said, Hunter and I were seeking our sustenance with a side order of climate control and iced tea, so we had a seat at one of the booths. I did, however, notice a large case of pies and cakes near the kitchen.

I ordered for us, our food came out and we enjoyed our meals (chicken quesadilla for Hunter and a Charlie Burger for myself). My vantage point gave me a good view of the kitchen, and I could see a woman in there dolloping…oh heavens, could that be meringue? The pie seed was growing in my head again, and I wanted some. I felt I needed to know about those pies. I really did. I decided that I could always just take home a fried pie, but I wanted a slice of whatever that lady had been working on. So I asked my waitress what pie was available and was told either chocolate or coconut. Hunter made the decision for us.

And it was a good decision. The pie that came out to us was on a nice slightly salty blind-baked crust. It had a moderate amount of coconut-infused meringue and one of the most perfectly conceived coconut custards I have ever consumed. The custard was packed with gentle flavor yet not too sweet, addictive even. Hunter insisted on having more than half of it and asked for more.

So I asked about the pies and the fried pies by the counter. Turns out they're made by two different ladies. Ms. Janie makes the fried pies, and they're individually wrapped to take with a traveler on the road (though I suspect that if you wanted to eat it there they'd heat it up for you). I requested a peach pie to take home once I heard it was made from local fruit.

I suppose my waitress had figured out we really liked pie, and she showed us another pie when she brought over the ticket. This was what had been under creation in the back. I am assuming from the conversation that the good lady I saw was Mrs. Rhonda Vaughn. And the pie? It was like nothing I'd ever encountered. It took two great pies and blended them together into something indescribably heavenly. It was a cherry cream cheese meringue pie. That's right. It was like a regular cherry cream cheese pie, except on top meringue had been piled and it had been baked together.

Fried pies by the register at Hillbilly Hideout in Ozark. *Kat Robinson.*

Well, I was already stuffed and I already had a box of leftovers and a fried pie, but I ponied up and bought a slice of that cherry cream cheese meringue pie to take home with me. And I have to tell you, when I got up the next morning, I had it for breakfast and it was absolutely divine.

So…there's a little more to this story. When I was editing the photos for this piece, I noticed the sign on the pie case and clutched my chest a little. On the door it listed the different regular varieties, which included not only possum pie but also the elusive millionaire pie (which until now I've only found at pie walks and Furr's Cafeteria). I had a friend bring me that dang millionaire pie, and I loved it—every pineapple-spotted, pecan-topped morsel of it.

Apple pie at DeVito's Restaurant at Bear Creek Springs near Harrison. *Grav Weldon*.

PART IV

Pie in the Family

Traditions run deep when it comes to pie in Arkansas.

DeVito's Restaurant

DeVito's at Bear Creek Springs offers several family traditions and some good pie to boot.

U.S. 65 runs from Clayton, Louisiana, through the Mississippi River Delta all the way up to Little Rock, across Missouri and Iowa up to Albert Lea, Minnesota. The highway used to be a long meandering path between Conway, Arkansas, and Springfield, Missouri—two lanes of twists, turns, inclines and declines spanning half a state. On its curves it held rock shops, quilt stores, smokehouses, fruit stands and every sort of roadside attraction. There were places to stop to view grand vistas, little quaint towns with old full-service gas stations, bluffs and waterfalls along roadsides and cute country-clad motels. Over the years, the kinks have been knocked out of the roadway as it has been improved to three- and even four-lane sections. The curves have been bypassed, in some areas numerous times.

One particular section of U.S. 65 north of Harrison has seen two bypasses in the past thirty years. The first, in 1982, moved the highway less than half a mile to the west, but it was enough to change things drastically for one Boone County family. The second just recently moved the highway farther to the west.

But the DeVito family won't give up. The fifth generation of DeVito cooks still prepares some of the best Italian specialties you can find in Arkansas right along Bear Creek Springs and the family trout farm, all these years later.

DeVito's Restaurant. *Grav Weldon.*

Joe DeVito. *Grav Weldon.*

The history reaches back several generations. On the DeVito side of the family there was Jim DeVito, an army man born in Wisconsin who grew up in Illinois. He served in the European theater during World War II. His first stateside posting afterward was at North Little Rock's Camp Robinson, where he met his future wife, Mary Alice Raney. She was a student at Baptist Hospital. They married in 1947, and when Jim DeVito retired in 1970 after twenty-nine years of service, they settled in Harrison.

Mary Alice's dad was Albert Raney Sr. He had himself a couple of big attractions up north of Jasper, a trout farm and a cave called Mystic Cavern that he showed people around. In 1966, he sold the trout farm and cave to an up-and-coming enterprise called Dogpatch USA. The Raney family continued to operate that trout farm until the attraction closed in 1993.

Mr. Raney also owned a little patch called Bear Creek Springs along U.S. 65. He had blasted the rock where the springs tumbled out and created another trout farm. When Jim and Mary Alice DeVito came back to Harrison in 1970, he gave them the farm to run and keep. They ran it with Mary's brother Gene quite successfully, building it up into a great attraction that was a must-stop for travelers on the Little Rock–to-Springfield route. In his retirement and with a crop of boys to feed, Jim also opened an antique store.

This was the first time the highway ran away from the DeVitos. For so many years, traffic had brought people whirring by the trout farm, right on the shoulder of the road and so easy to see. They stopped in droves to cast a line and reel in dinner. But when Bear Creek Springs was bypassed in 1982, they stopped stopping.

Business for the trout farm shrank—out of sight, out of mind. Sure, there were signs to direct people down into the hollow below the new roadway, but there were also signs going the other way for U.S. 62, which took travelers to Eureka Springs; signs for Silver Dollar City, the growing theme park in Branson just across the Missouri border; signs for acts such as the Baldknobbers and the Presleys along Highway 76.

Well, it was time for a change. In 1986, with the four boys back home and full partners in the enterprise, the DeVitos opened a restaurant across the road from the trout farm. It became an overnight success. People would drive in from miles around to come eat fresh trout and fabulous Italian dishes in the little restaurant over the antique store and rock shop. Some would come and fish at the farm and have their catches cooked up fresh, but far more came just to eat and experience a fabulous Italian experience in the Ozarks.

And the popularity was well earned. The men held court in the kitchen, cooking fish and making sides, bread and dessert from scratch. Their rich tomato-strong sauce became famous, as did their overstuffed ravioli. The restaurant drew in business so fast that two years after opening, oldest son James picked up and started a second restaurant in Eureka Springs, which was also an instant hit. And in the late 1990s, a third DeVito's was opened at Big Cedar Lodge near Branson.

That last restaurant was fortuitous. In 2000, the original DeVito's at Bear Creek Springs was destroyed by fire. Business still continued at Big Cedar Lodge, but there was a decision to be made. Brothers Steve, Chris and Joe made the decision—they had to rebuild. Fourteen months later, they were open once again in a beautiful new facility twice as large as the old one. It thrived from the moment it opened its doors.

But the highway wasn't done with the DeVitos. The late aughts brought controversy to folks all along the Harrison-to-Branson corridor, with the coming of a four-lane replacement for the major highway that connected the two cities. The new road was given the U.S. 65 designation, the old road became a series of local loops along the way and DeVito's Restaurant and trout farm were that much farther from the hubbub of traffic.

Still, it persists. Sure, business took a hit, but locals still come all the time. And the restaurant is still filled with DeVitos—the boys have had children of their own, and most of the employees are some relation.

But what does that have to do with pie? Well, there are many family traditions the DeVitos still practice. Each day, a member of the clan goes down to the trout farm and catches the trout for the day. Each morning, someone comes in and makes bread. And each day, Steve DeVito bakes up the desserts they'll offer that day. The chocolate bourbon pecan pie might be the most alcohol-soaked dessert in Boone County, with a generous portion of Canada Mist in its makeup. The rich pecan custard is judiciously enhanced by the chocolate and served up on a soft biscuit-like crust.

Still, hands down, the best pie at DeVito's has to be the apple pie. The almost phyllo dough layered crust is redolent of butter. The apples are pliant, recently picked, never canned, almost pear-like in flavor and firmness, sweet apples instead of tart. With homemade-style golden vanilla ice cream, it's ambrosial.

It's amazing how peaceful a visit is to Bear Creek Springs these days. Without the constant stream of U.S. 65 traffic, the little community is quiet. The same old bridge just north of the Springs is still there, probably unchanged since 1982. Up on the old highway, the signs still point into the hollow. And out on the new four-lane, there's a sign that says just where to turn to head down to the trout farm. If you're along the way, it's worth a stop in.

Bourbon pecan pie at DeVito's Restaurant. *Grav Weldon*.

You'll find DeVito's Restaurant and the trout farm at Bear Creek Springs by heading north on U.S. 65 from Harrison to Old U.S. 65 north of town. Veer right and go a short distance for the next right-hand turn. The restaurant will be a block down on the left; the trout farm is across the street to the right.

Chip's Barbecue

The longtime Little Rock barbecue joint is the city's best-kept pie secret.

It can be argued that the best pie in Little Rock can only be found by the locals. After all, Chip's Barbecue along West Markham isn't exactly a household name. But the family does make some of the most highly sought-after pies in the city.

The place was started back in 1961 by Tom Chipman and his wife, Tina. Over the years, their kids have run the place, keeping it as charming and traditional as it ever was. You can still go in and sit at a green vinyl upholstered booth between those wood-paneled walls, order up ribs or nachos or the Muffin Special and shoot the bull with your buds.

Mr. Chip, as he was called, passed away in June 2012. His daughter Kara has always been really good to me. Back when I was writing my first cover story for the *Arkansas Times*, she let me come in and photograph pies—for over an hour, pie after pie after pie—for which I was eternally grateful.

See, Chip's pies are Little Rock's sweetest secret. You have to know about Chip's to have some of that pie, but folks who know about it guard it and keep it to themselves and order pies weeks in advance for holidays. There are cream pies galore—banana and lemon and coconut and chocolate, and sometimes sweet potato or pumpkin, too. There are variations, like the marvelous chocolate walnut pie. And then there are the cheesecakes—big, four-inch-thick affairs served up plain or with raspberry sauce or strawberries or chocolate or nuts. And there's pecan pie and seasonal pies

Lemon, chocolate and banana cream pies at Chip's Barbecue in Little Rock. *Kat Robinson*.

Lemon cream pie at Chip's Barbecue. *Kat Robinson*.

like strawberry or blueberry. Every one of them made from scratch from a family recipe.

If you are from around here and you are smart, you order pies from Chip's at least a week before any major holiday. They make a few extra pies, but not enough for the onslaught of folks who seek out a good pie when time grows too short to make one at home.

Dew-Baby's

Dew-Baby's is all about family.

Big families aren't the norm anymore. Used to be a family of ten or more would be common, since families needed to be big to run big homesteads and the like. Not these days.

How about a couple that had seven kids just over a year after they got married—and then went on to have fourteen more? No, it's not some sensational crazy multiples story. It's the story of the Jefferys out of tiny Casscoe, Arkansas. George and Girstine Jeffery started off shortly after their marriage as surrogate parents to seven children. They then went on to build their own family, having ten girls and four boys along the way. Girstine was known as "Dew-Baby," and it's after her that this little restaurant in Stuttgart is named.

I went on a Friday to seek out something fantastical—an egg custard pie of some renown. I was very happy to see it on the menu. Egg custard is one of those great cultural pies that doesn't seem to ever have caught on with the frou-frou set. It's very pedestrian, very rural…and very comforting. A good egg custard pie is filling, too.

We pulled up to the well-used building on Michigan Street (next door to, of all things, a gyro shack) and went on in. Dew-Baby's is two separate dining rooms: the one you walk into with the counter and the buffet bar and the one on the side where the restrooms are. It was 11:00 a.m. dead on, and we were apparently the first customers of the day.

I talked with the ladies a bit before ordering that pie. They're all daughters (and one daughter-in-law) of Dew-Baby, and they work together lovingly.

Thing is, even though I was planning to dine somewhere else (I had a busy day planned), I couldn't resist the scent that struck me when I walked through the door: fried chicken. Pan-fried chicken at that, the sort that comes from a cast-iron skillet. Oh, I was having lunch.

I asked for dark meat chicken with my meat-and-three—the two sisters working the counter that day mentioned they always preferred the breast meat, I suspect since they make theirs nice and juicy—but I got my dark meat chicken and three sides. I chose French fries, baked beans and a lettuce and mayonnaise salad. My other choices were corn on the cob and hush puppies, and fried catfish for the main course.

And of course I ordered up that egg custard pie. I was going to have me some of that. Desserts are $2.50 each, well worth it. The other choices that day were sweet potato pie, pineapple upside-down cake, chocolate cake and cream cheese cake.

My photographer and I had a seat while we waited for the plate to be made up. We sipped briefly on iced tea before one of the sisters brought the plate to the table. It smelled heavenly.

The fried chicken—okay, we're going to have to put some debate to this. I have eaten what I thought was the best fried chicken in the state, which has been either at AQ Chicken House in Springdale or at the Monte Ne Inn Chicken Restaurant. This chicken—wait for the blasphemy here—was *better*. It had the tenderness and flavor of being buttermilk-soaked, a very light bit of spicing that I felt had to have included some lemon pepper, it was juicy, it was flavorful, it was tender and it was golden. And yet still it was nothing in comparison to the pie I was about to receive.

The side dishes were odd but good. The baked beans were of the same sort you normally find in pork 'n' beans but were flavored instead with brown sugar and ground beef, almost identical to the Settler's Beans my mom makes each Thanksgiving. The fries were about average. The prepared salad was interesting—bacon (which I avoided, being allergic to pork), shredded cheddar cheese, iceberg lettuce, cucumber, slices of hard-boiled egg and English peas in what tasted like a version of Miracle Whip.

And then there was the egg custard pie. It was pretty. It had sliced clean, indicative of a balanced hand in its construction. It was substantial. I mean, well, it's like eating an omelet as far as the cholesterol and calories go, frankly. But I tell you, I was won over by three facts. The pie was created with a homemade, folded-over flour pastry that was slightly salty. The custard was homogenous and perfect—very firm and very smooth. And the top had been browned to an almost crème brulee perfection. I have yet to find a better pie.

We visited with one of the sisters, who came over to talk with us about the Lord and how He takes care of us, no matter our troubles. It was a bit of good conversation to have while enjoying a good meal, and we saw it repeated with the only other first-time visitor who came in the door. Regulars they all greeted by name, asking about families and how work was going and all sorts of things like that.

We had to finish up and get on the road, but I made a note I need to return, probably on a Tuesday when all the vegetables like the PurpleHull peas and such are out. I was thrilled to finally find a really great restaurant in town, and I'm looking forward to going back and hearing more about this neat family.

Turns out there's a book on the matter called *Ten Sisters* by Rose Stovall, one of the sisters, a collection of stories from each of the sisters about their mom and dad and growing up in Casscoe. I'm going to seek this book out and read it. I think it might give me more insight into life in the Delta.

The Lunchbox

The Lunchbox is Searcy's answer to great family dining…and pie.

Most every Arkansas town has a thoroughfare that's lined with every sort of business that stretches from one end of the city to the other. In Little Rock, it's Markham Street (though it used to be University Avenue). In Conway, it's Oak Street. Hot Springs has Central Avenue, and Fort Smith has Rogers Avenue. And in Searcy, it's Race Street.

Along Race Street you'll find a large yellow-painted façade on the north side of the road, right near where you turn to head to the fairgrounds. It's only been open since May 2011, but the Lunchbox may just have the sort of staying power a restaurant like that needs. You see, it runs on family—not just great family restaurants but also the idea of a growing family.

The Vanwinkles, who own the place, used to run a catering concession called Jelly Bellies. They had a dream to do something bigger, and when they saw the old empty A&W building up for sale, they decided that's what they were going to do with their tax refund check. However, someone beat them to it and opened a restaurant in that location before they could get the money together.

You know, sometimes things just work out the way they should. About the time that refund made it to the Vanwinkles, the "For Sale" sign reappeared on the lot, and it was quickly theirs.

When you walk in, you'll find a dining room full of light, followed by an ordering bar where you can either choose a burger or sandwich, pick up a

Inside the Lunchbox in Searcy. *Grav Weldon.*

Strawberry icebox pie at the Lunchbox. *Grav Weldon*.

Coconut fried pie at the Lunchbox. *Grav Weldon*.

piece of fudge or pay to have the daily buffet, which always features at least two types of meat and nine different vegetables. And, of course, there's pie.

The recipes for all those neat dishes and side dishes, fudge and pie come from family—particularly Joy Vanwinkle's grandmother. They're served up in an atmosphere that's meant to remind you what it's like to dine in a country kitchen.

Those pies? You can get a fried pie just about any day in one of several flavors. The coconut fried pie is just an absolute delight, buttery to a fault and packed with hot filling. But it's one of the sliced pies that truly captured my heart. It's the strawberry icebox pie, which, quite honestly, is more of a strawberry cream pie with a rich strawberry-tinted cream cheese layer, sweet local strawberries and whipped cream. It's a Sunday-go-to-meeting pie, and it's going to become a quick classic around town.

Blackberry fried pie at the Hurley House Café in Hazen. *Kat Robinson.*

PART V

The Detta, Dominion of the Fried Pie

Fried pies, fried pies everywhere

Sweet Treat of the Delta

A tour of eastern Arkansas and its fried pies

The folded-over pie is nothing new in this world. Like many food traditions, the idea of taking something and wrapping it in dough dates back to antiquity. Putting something inside something else made of flour goes back to the Romans for sure, probably the Greeks and quite possibly even further back than that.

In the Middle Ages, that flour dough wrapped around meat or vegetables was called a coffin (same name as a box you put a body in, but quite a different thing in practice). It was a hand-formed vessel for food made from dough, and it was usually an inch thick or more. The dough kept the contents intact and prevented them from burning. The dough left over from the process was thrown out to the poor to eat; it was hard, sometimes burned and barely edible. Somewhere along the way, someone got the idea of "waste not, want not" in their head and figured out how to make the crust edible, likely with the introduction of metal cookware into the kitchen. After all, it's not like medieval chefs had Pyrex and Calphalon.

Shortly before the Renaissance, the English served up what they called a Grete Pye. It was a pastry filled with meat (beef and poultry were the norm), dried fruit and spices. Fruit pies became popular, but it wasn't until about the time of the Revolutionary War that sweetened fruit pies came into fashion.

In New England, another type of pie developed: pasties (pronounced PAH-stees), big hand pies full of something savory like stew. There's even a

Chocolate fried pie at Cotham's Mercantile in Scott. *Kat Robinson.*

variation in New England where home chefs would tuck a bit of jam or some spiced and sweetened fruit into the end of the big pies. They were easy to transport and made the perfect working-man food.

Which brings me to the fried pies of the Delta. See, fried pies can be found all over Arkansas, from fine dining establishments like Capital Bar and Grill in Little Rock to barbecue joints like Nick's BBQ and Catfish in Carlisle to roadside diners like Ray's Dairy Maid in Barton to gas stations like Rison Country Store. The deepest saturation of places I found to procure fried pies is in the Arkansas Delta.

The expanse covers a third of the state, a sweeping plain that stretches along the eastern border onward without interruption, save for Crowley's Ridge. It comes in as far as Little Rock and Dumas and Bald Knob. If you look at a highway map, you can see its outline—just trace down U.S. 67 from Corning to the center of the state, then follow west on U.S. 65 all the way down to Eudora. It's a vast, flat land squared off into soybean and rice fields, cotton, corn, sorghum and winter wheat, punctuated by crescents and patches of trees and a few leftover sections of swamp. Outside the banks of the White, Black, Cache and Arkansas Rivers, the streams seem straight. There are reasons for this.

Most of what we consider to be the Delta today was swampland in the nineteenth century and before. It was barely inhabitable mosquito-breeding wetlands, hard to navigate and difficult to see potential in. But it was rich, too, with topsoil one hundred feet deep. The pioneers of this land were men who dug ditches to create farms. They started by scooping out the earth and making a new route for the myriad little streams here and there and then utilizing those redirected water sources to irrigate crops on land left dry by those redirections.

If you fly over the Arkansas Delta today, you see a patchwork quilt below, blocks of green and brown and sometimes the reflection of water from soaking rice fields, punctuated by stands of trees near canals and streams laced with highways and county roads. The strongly forested Crowley's Ridge breaks up the area, a loess formation rising up to two hundred feet above the Mississippi River Alluvial Plain. It's the lone ridge between Memphis and Little Rock, stretching from around Helena–West Helena up to the Missouri border.

Farming is stronger here than in the rest of the state. And there's a culture to it. It used to be a family culture—families had their hundreds of acres and farmed them the old-fashioned way: by creating more family. The kids were raised and they did their chores and worked the land and eventually had kids of their own. Until late in the twentieth century, lunches were the sort of thing you either went back to the main house to eat with your folks or something tied in a handkerchief—a lump of cheese and a chunk of bread, a piece of ham or something from last night's dinner. Later on it'd be a sandwich or a can of something like sardines.

Thing is, just like in the rest of the world, a combination of communication and mechanization expanded the knowledge base and encouraged folks to head to the city, just as the size of families began to shrink. Maybe there weren't a dozen mouths to feed three times a day. Maybe one spouse worked the land while the other worked in a plant or at a shop. Times changed.

I'm a city girl, but I was raised by folks who came from the bottomlands of southwest Arkansas. I missed out on the farmer culture until I was done with college and in my first television job at a station in Jonesboro, KAIT. It was the only TV station in town, an ABC affiliate, in the biggest city in the Arkansas Delta—the hub of life in northeast Arkansas. And it was a culture shock. There were some pieces of city life to be found, with a little shopping, some parks, a movie theater—but if you really wanted the city experience,

A basket of fried pies at Dairy King in Portia. *Grav Weldon.*

you hopped on U.S. 63 and headed down to Memphis. Jonesboro was, at the time, a little country town in big city clothes.

In my three years there, I explored. I was in my early twenties, and what was I going to do when I wasn't working? I'd get in my car and drive. And between stopping in at little diners around the area and by covering the agriculture beat in the morning newscast I produced, I learned about farming in the Delta. I will never be an expert, but I could meet and begin to understand the people I saw in those country diners, the sort of folks who would show up to a rally for Marion Berry (the state representative for the area at the time), the sort who spent a lot of time on a combine.

These sorts of folks would get up at the butt-crack of dawn to begin their jobs, usually showering and dressing before the first light of morning. They would likely eat a quick breakfast at the house and get out to work, whether it was to plow or harvest soybeans, rice, winter wheat or any other crop, or head out to market to sell what they brought in from the fields.

About 11:00 a.m., they would leave the fields for lunch. They would seek out communion in the form of others to bump elbows with around a table, usually in a diner or a country store here or there. A typical lunch would involve these men (and they were, almost to a T, all men) arriving at a restaurant, gathering around a table and chewing the fat with others of their ilk. There might be a waitress, and there might even be a menu, but for these men it would be a matter of sitting down and accepting whatever the lunch plate happened to be, usually with coffee but sometimes with a Coke and a smile.

And when the meal was done and it was time to head back, each man would head to the counter to settle the tab. Next to the register there would be something sweet in Saran wrap, a cookie bar or a piece of cake—or a fried pie. Each man would pick up one of those fried pies and move it over by the ticket he'd put down in front of the lady at the register, and she'd quietly ring it up with his lunch. Money exchanged, fried pie in hand, the guy would be right out the door and on with his work.

See, the idea that began with dumplings and pasties and such has embedded itself in Delta life. The hand pie is a natural for someone to pick up on the go. It's just as popular with truckers and travelers as it is with these hearty folk who sow the fields.

But why fried? You could view it as a product of refrigeration. There are other dessert items that can be picked up and taken with you somewhere but few that can be batched and frozen and then later cooked quickly. It takes just a few minutes to cook a fried pie, and if it's been frozen it doesn't matter—the frying process that crisps the dough and turns it golden brown melts it and makes molten whatever is contained within.

A Delta Pie Trail

Experiencing a Delta fried pie trail in a single day

If you head south and east of Little Rock, you can experience a day's worth of pie and still get back home in time for dinner. The slice of land that spreads from the Timberlands to the Arkansas River's own delta is rich in the soil and populated by restaurants that specialize in the fried pie.

Your first stop is actually for fuel. Heading south on U.S. 63 from Pine Bluff and almost to Rison, you'll find the Rison Country Store, a little gray service station on the right-hand side of the road. It's the sort of place where you stock provisions before heading out into the woods or on the river or the road. And right by the register, you'll find individually wrapped fried pies just about any time they're open.

The pies are handmade each day. They're a biscuit-crust sort of pie with a thick, flaky crust. The fried apple is about the best—local apples stewed on the stove top with spices, spooned into the crust and folded over, deep fried and sprinkled with cinnamon and sugar, a trucker's friend of a hand pie.

Head down U.S. 63 a while longer and take a left on Highway 114, and it'll take you to Star City. Just off Highway 425 on the south side of town, you'll find an interesting little village that includes a jewelry shop, a barbershop, a taxidermy place, a leather-working shop, a small engine repair place and a selection of restaurants, including one that specializes in barbecue and another that does catfish. This is Country Village, run by members of a single small church.

Rison Country Store in Rison. *Grav Weldon*.

Pies and cakes in the case at Country Village Bakery near Star City. *Grav Weldon*.

Apricot fried pie at Country Village Bakery. *Grav Weldon*.

You'll want to head to the bakery, which offers great breads, cakes and pies five days a week. I'm not talking about just one or two pies. On my visit, I discovered everything from a chocolate caramel nut pie to a caramel apple mini pie, whole pecan pies and sugar-free pecan pies, plain apple pies and peach pies. There are also fried pies, big six- to eight-inch crescents made with a doughnut-style crust, glazed like a doughnut and filled with rich local fruit, as well as chocolate and vanilla.

Strangely enough, while the Country Village Bakery makes its own fried pies, it also fries pies for the Amish and Country Store in Dermott. At that store, the filling and dough are made, the pies are formed and frozen. They're sent to Country Village to be fried in the kitchen and then sent right back to be sold in the store. They come in a large variety of flavors. Apricot fried pies are strongly flavored affairs with big chunks of rehydrated fruit within; blueberry fried pies are mellow and almost suckable in their consistency. The pies, to me, seem like large versions of the old Hostess fried pies when it comes to the glazed crust, but the home-turned filling is clean and fresh and flavorful.

From there, turn back out on Highway 425 and head south to Monticello, where you can either wait a while and pick up a grand fried pie at Ray's (go

Piggy Sue's in Monticello. *Grav Weldon*.

for the chocolate) or at Piggy Sue's (try the apple), both on the main highway. Then double back and head to Dermott on Highway 35. Just past town, you'll hit U.S. 65, and that's where you'll find the Amish and Country Store I mentioned before. No, it's not run by actual Amish folk. But it is run by a sweet family that shares a lot of baked goods, jams, cheeses and furniture in their store for sale. If you're making the Little Rock to New Orleans run, it's a must-stop.

Head out north through McGehee and on to Dumas, but turn on Pickens Road just before you get there. That left-hand turn and a quarter mile will take you to the restaurant on the old Pickens farm. There, if you make it between 11:00 a.m. and 2:00 p.m. Monday through Friday, you can rub elbows with local farmers and the occasional tourist and enjoy baked or fried chicken or pork chops or whatever they're cooking up that day. If you have lunch, you *must* get the squash casserole, and you should certainly consider picking up a fried pie for the road. And if you decide to dawdle, the Pickens Commissary pecan pie is a slice of home, while its fresh strawberry is one of the finest in the state.

Ray's Dairy Maid

The Arkansas Delta doesn't get its share of culinary media coverage. There are just a couple of places I can think of that have received just due. One is the James Beard award–winning Jones' Bar B Q in Marianna. The other received notice thanks to Alton Brown and *Feasting on Asphalt*. If you've ever sat down at Ray's Dairy Maid in Barton and had a slice of pie, you know what I'm talking about.

It could be any of a hundred different drive-ins around the state. Inside you see the same sort of memorabilia, the same whiteboard listing the specials, the same sort of tabletop with business cards shoved up under the glass.

What makes it different are Deane Cavette's pies. Her fried pies are delicate and light, the crust a flaky barely-there complement to fresh fillings. Any fried pie at Ray's is a good bet.

Cavette says pie making didn't come naturally to her. "When I got married, I could not make a pie to save my neck," she'll tell you. "First one I made was an apple pie, when I was first married, that we couldn't eat. And we threw it out the back door and the dog wouldn't eat it. I taught myself my pies…I make what people ask for."

And they do ask for those pies, no matter how big their britches are. "One afternoon a few years ago, there were a bunch of college-aged kids that came here in an RV, and they asked about the pie. They tried it, and they made some phone calls. Then this guy comes riding up on a motorcycle, walks in and says, 'I'm here for the pie.' And that was Alton Brown." The

Nana Deane's Coconut Pecan Pie at Ray's Dairy Maid in Barton. *Grav Weldon.*

popular Food Network star was filming for his *Feasting on Asphalt* series; Ray's Dairy Maid was the only stop he included in Arkansas.

Cavette doesn't make the pies every day anymore; a bout with illness in the winter of 2011 set her back a bit. Today, she checks in on the restaurant regularly with her husband, Ray, and her recipes are still whipped up—the fried pies outside the restaurant with those same recipes, the pan pies right in the store.

That being said, it's a real tragedy to leave the place without having a slice of Nana Deane's coconut pecan pie. It's as if a pecan praline knocked up a coconut meringue pie—sweet yet salty and oh so rich.

Nana Deane's Coconut Pecan Pie

10½ ounces granulated sugar

3 large whole eggs

2 ounces unsalted butter, melted

4 ounces buttermilk

3 ounces sweetened coconut flakes

3 ounces pecans, chopped (approximately ¾ cup)

1 tablespoon all-purpose flour

1 teaspoon vanilla extract

pinch salt

1 pie crust (pre-baked)

Preheat oven to 350°.

In a large mixing bowl, combine the sugar, eggs, melted butter, buttermilk, coconut, pecans, flour, vanilla and salt. Pour into a nine-inch pre-baked pie crust.

Bake for 45 minutes or until the pie is golden brown and the center is barely set.

Cool for 40 to 45 minutes before serving.

Big John's Shake Shack

Most fried pies come in half-moon shapes. Some come in fold-overs, which are rectangular. At Big John's Shake Shack in Marion, fried pies come in triangular wedges, a moist glistening fork-crimped fold-over crust packed with filling. The best of the lot is the caramel apple fried pie, filled with big slices of syrupy slurpable apples, encapsulated in a goo redolent of cinnamon and state fairs, hot and molten and just absolutely perfect.

The Shake Shack's been around since 1977, a local icon that's now served a couple generations of sweet teeth. Loretta Tacker has been making pies there since she and her husband, John Wayne Tacker, started the place up. He may be gone, but she's still busy cranking out one great pie after another. She keeps a fried pie case right by the register filled with caramel apple, regular apple, peach, cherry and chocolate wedges. More than that, she always has another pie case packed with whole pies she's managed to whip up. She even has a few she keeps in the icebox. They're listed on whiteboards and blackboards, and they go on and on—chocolate, apple, cherry, lemon icebox, peanut butter, Tang icebox (I am not making that up), cherry cream cheese…

And then there was the hot fudge pie. I'm violating the rule of pie by including it here. More brownie than pie, it's actually baked in a pie pan and has a little bit of a crust, so it qualifies. Right? Well, it has crust the same way a brownie does. But there's something about it, something slightly molten and completely delicious, that's allowing me to overlook the obvious flaw in that pie argument.

One of the pie cases at Big John's Shake Shack in Marion. *Grav Weldon.*

Cotham's Mercantile

Everyone must eventually make the pilgrimage to Cotham's Mercantile.

If there was just one restaurant you could put a finger on that has attracted people from all walks of life, that's interested travelers and intrigued politicians, that's brought everyone from ditch diggers to debutantes out to rural Arkansas, that restaurant would be Cotham's Mercantile.

Famed for its Hubcap Burgers and featured on nationwide food shows and in magazines all over the place, Cotham's looks the part. It's a burger and plate lunch joint housed in an old community store perched on the side of Horseshoe Lake in the small town of Scott, which lies between North Little Rock and Keo on Highway 165. It has over the years become so popular with the legislative crowd that a second location (Cotham's in the City) is offered in downtown Little Rock, just blocks from the state capitol.

Cotham's has earned its reputation. The burgers have a familiar flavor, and you can purchase the spice to take home with you. The fried green tomatoes are noteworthy, and the onion rings are phenomenal. In fact, the food is so beloved that very few actually make it to the fried pies.

Those pies are hand-rolled, fork-crimped affairs, rounded like your pocket. The dough is flaky and slightly layered, light and unsweetened, a tiny bit chewy. Inside, your filling of choice is always hot. Traditionally they're served up fancy style with ice cream, but whipped cream is also an acceptable substitute.

The food likely as not tastes the same at both locations, and the city location is decorated with the campaign signs of one hundred different politicians from over the years. But the drive out to Scott is restful, the quaint surroundings of the old store and its collection of doodled-upon napkins is charming and the post-consumption drive down Arkansas 161 to the pecan grove and back can restore your peace with the world.

Poppy's Diner and Dairy King

Poppy's Diner in Lepanto and Dairy King in Portia share a similar methodology.

Northeast Arkansas is the only place I have found in the state that incorporates cream cheese into its fried pies. And at both places, the pie is a fold-over. That's a rectangular pie, sort of like what McDonald's used to do when it fried pies.

In Lepanto, just a few blocks from where John Grisham's *Painted House* was filmed, you'll find a little place called Poppy's Diner at the end of a series of downtown buildings. Poppy's serves up burgers and sandwiches and some strange things too, like fried Oreos and "cry-baby" hot wings. And they do fried pies—coconut, apple, pecan and chocolate. The most popular is the cherry cream cheese pie, which you have to wait about twelve minutes for so they can fill it and fry it up right. It's what it sounds like—a cherry cream cheese pie filling inside a fold-over rectangular pie, sprinkled with powdered sugar. It's not all that large, but dang it's powerful.

Head down to Tyronza and then cut up and past Walnut Ridge on U.S. 63, and you come to a little spot in the road called Portia. When I saw that spot in the road—I am not kidding—it consisted of only a grocery store, a barbecue joint and the Dairy King, which serves not one but two types of fried pies. The one they make there is the strawberry cream cheese pie. Once again, it is a rectangular fold-over that takes time to cook up (order it with your burger) but packs a punch.

At the register, there are cold fried pies in a basket. Those come from the Ozark Kitchen out of Cave City, and they come in apple, raisin, blueberry, chocolate and whatnot. Many of the "cash register companion" pies in the area come from that little pie shop.

Batten's Bakery

A singular throwback to another generation at Batten's Bakery

Fried pies in Arkansas can come in many shapes, from the horseshoe crescents of Cotham's Mercantile to the fold-overs of Poppy's Diner, from the elongated half-rounds at Hillbilly Hideout to the perfect hemispheres of Ray's Dairy Maid and even to the triangular pies made at Big John's Shake Shack. But what's inside comes down to one of three things—a cream filling, a nut filling or a fruit filling.

But there's a fried pie creation that goes back a whole lot further. It's still being made the same way today as it was way back in 1954 in Paragould, at a place called Batten's Bakery.

Now, Batten's has been a family operation for a long time. The current owners, Mike and Bridgette Batten, took over in 2008. The bakery has always served up these pies and over the years has done doughnuts, cakes and even hot breakfast items. And you will indeed find fruit and custard pies at Batten's. I've had a few of them. They tend to be made with a sort of dough reminiscent of their doughnut dough, packed tight with custard or with a fruited filling of some sort. And they're good.

But the Old Fashioned is extraordinary.

See, way back when the place started, the Old Fashioned was, well, fashioned. It was and still is a round of dough crimped over with filling inside. The filling in this case is a blend of cocoa, sugar and butter—and nothing else. The frying of this pie makes the middle a little soft, but it's hard

The filling of an Old Fashioned chocolate fried pie at Batten's Bakery in Paragould is made from cocoa, sugar and butter. *Kat Robinson*.

to describe. It's not a custard. It's more like…well, like the sort of frosting you might find on a cake at a church social. Or a dry fudge. Or…

The filling crumbles. It's solid but not too hard. It's sweet but not overbearing, and it's perfect. And it's something you could have found in almost any Arkansas kitchen two and three generations back. Of all the places I have been, this is the only place where you can still purchase an Old Fashioned. When in Paragould, make your way there.

Ms. Lena's Whole and Fried Pies

The fried pie that started my search for the sweet truth

My personal fried pie journey began back in my television days. I worked at Today's THV in Little Rock as the senior morning show producer for eight years. At the time, I thought I'd be in TV for the rest of my days.

We'd have guests in every morning, and one morning we had in Ms. Lena Rice and her kids, talking about fried pies. And those pies—well, they made an impression on me. Unlike any other fried pies I'd ever encountered, these were made with a marvelous thin but strong flour dough, and they were overstuffed. *Very* overstuffed. I knew I'd be heading out to DeValls Bluff to pick up more later.

When I left TV in September 2007, I started thinking about what I was going to do. I had assumed I'd be going into public relations, but within a few weeks, I was writing for small publications around town. I'd also started up my own blog, "Tie Dye Travels," just to keep my writing sharp. I shared different places I went around the state.

Well, I went out to Ms. Lena's shop, and I talked with Viv Barnhill, Lena's daughter. And that started something. I took home my pies, wrote about them and moved on a bit. But a few days later, I noticed a swift uptick in the number of hits I got on my blog. Turns out, Max Brantley over at the *Arkansas Times* saw the piece and decided to link it to "Eat Arkansas," the weekly paper's food blog.

This was the beginning of everything that happened in my writing life. From that notice, I picked up more of the little publications, and I contributed more blogs that were linked from the *Times* site. About eleven months later (I was about eight months pregnant at the time), Max sent me a note and asked if I'd be interested in writing "Eat Arkansas" for a modest fee. Of course I jumped at it. That led to more work, first with Lonely Planet, then with Serious Eats and then with myriad other publications. My work made it to *Food Network Magazine*, my photos made it to *Food and Wine* and my reputation spread. It can be argued that all that work landed me the job I have today with the Arkansas Department of Parks and Tourism.

And it was all over a little pie, a little hand pie. And this is the story of that pie, how it disappeared and how it came back.

Ms. Lena's Pie Shop sits on the side of Highway 33, about a block south of U.S. 70 in the relaxed little village of DeValls Bluff. When I first made that trip in the fall of 2007, Vivian Barnhill and Carl Rice made a practice of getting up early every Saturday morning and working up about eight hundred fried pies. They'd make up the filling, and then Viv would make up the dough and Carl would roll it out. They'd bake from the wee hours and through the shop's opening at 9:00 a.m. Twelve hours out of every Saturday they made the little pies, turning out six flavors that would be picked up singly, in dozens and in big boxes by people who came from up to a couple hours' drive in every direction to pick them up. They were that good.

That one morning when I stepped out of my car at the little house, I was overwhelmed with the scent of baking pies. The smell of fresh-baked dough and fruit hung in the air outside the establishment like a tasty cloak of goodness. It made my mouth water.

Inside, there wasn't much room on the customer side of the counter, which held nothing more than a guest book and a register, just about enough room for three people to stand at the counter. The wall (then as now) was covered with articles from *Southern Living*, photos from Today's THV and pictures of Ms. Lena herself. Viv's daughter Kim took the orders at the counter.

The regular flavors were apricot, apple, chocolate, coconut and peach. That particular day, the extra flavor was cherry. Each came wrapped in a paper napkin, and if you ordered a half dozen or more, they came in a clamshell box with the lid carefully and barely closed with just a piece of masking tape. The pies were almost always still hot and fresh because so many people came through that Viv and Carl could barely keep up with the orders. The pies were still steaming, and I had to put mine in the backseat so they'd be too far away for me to grab and consume as I drove home.

Fried pies on the shelves at Ms. Lena's in DeValls Bluff. *Kat Robinson*.

Ms. Lena Barnhill. *Viv Barnhill*.

Each pie was wonderful. The chocolate pies were creamy and surprisingly light, with a filling reminiscent of a good meringue pie instead of the pudding that so many places use. The cherry was a pleasantly light filling with a hint of maraschino. Coconut pies were rich and slightly cool in the middle, with big hunks of flakes. Apricot pies were pungently sweet and tasty, like the best preserves. Peach pies were smooth and sweet and chunky, and apple pies were full of slightly crisp tart bites in creamy syrup.

Now, as I'd mentioned before, I'd had Ms. Lena's pies so I knew about fantastic otherworldly flavors like pecan and lemon and peanut butter. I'd even had the strawberry pies that came along only during a particular part of the summer. And I loved the Woodpecker—a chocolate pie with a dab of cherry in the middle, named in honor of the ivory-billed woodpecker that's supposed to have been sighted in the area (and which remains an object of contention in these parts). Each pie was sealed in a crispy crust both fork-tender and light and amazingly grease-free.

Viv told me about all the different people who had come through. She told me about a gentleman from New Zealand who came over to the States just to look around. Seems he had retired early and wanted to see the world. She said when he came to Ms. Lena's, he asked for a bowl of milk. She asked why, and he told her it was to soak the pie. She handed him a pie wrapped in a napkin and explained how we do it around here—and he sure caught on quick. He'd inhaled three pies before he left the building!

Vivian and Carl came to running the business after the passing of their mother. Ms. Lena Rice was something else. She ran the shop for several years out of her house (that's where the pies are still sold) and had a bunch of regulars who would come buy pies by the dozens. But over the years, her health failed, and she wasn't able to do it anymore. Before she left this good earth, she made the kids promise they'd continue the tradition.

They did—for a while. Viv also made whole pies, and her half-and-half chocolate coconut pie became a thing of legend, one side a fantastic coconut meringue with creamy filling and flaky bits of coconut throughout, the other a smooth sweet chocolate with a traditional meringue. I loved getting the piece of the pie with both in it.

But after a while, things got tough, and they had to shut down the shop. For a summer, there were no pies, fried or otherwise. It made me blue.

Then they got started again selling the whole pies. Well, they were always good pies, but I missed those fried pies. I knew they took a lot of work and probably didn't make them any money considering the labor involved, but dang if I didn't want them back.

Viv Barnhill at Ms. Lena's. *Grav Weldon*.

One day, Viv sent me a message and asked if I'd like to come see fried pies being made. Well, of course I would. It was a June day in 2011, and though I'd come through town in February for a half-and-half, I was dying for a hand pie. I got there and business was picking up, but Viv ushered me through the kitchen door and proceeded to show me around and let me shoot the hell out of the place. And that's how I got to chronicle how the pies are made.

Start with good fillings—no preservatives, just what's supposed to be in the pie. For instance, the apple pie filling is just chopped-up apples in their own juices with a few spices. The chocolate custard is made from scratch. And those apricots—well, we'll talk about them in a minute.

Carl was in charge of making the crust, that special recipe that Ms. Lena shared only with her children. The dough was rolled into equal portions in balls. He took each one and smashed it with his hand and then rolled it out with a small roller. He'd flip it and roll again, four or five times. How could you tell it was thin enough? When a fully rolled-out crust is held up to the light, you can see through it.

Carl would pile those crusts in a floured stack, and Viv would take each one, put it in a crimper, dollop filling into the crust and crimp it over. She would then take the pie and put it directly into the fryer, where it would cook up a good minute or two. Out of the fryer, each pie went onto a wooden rack to drain.

Now, because those crusts are thin, there was sometimes a blowout, and the rule in the shop was that if there was a blow-out, that pie had to be eaten behind the counter instead of sold. Funny how the chocolate pies were the most likely to blow out. The apricot didn't blow out that often—probably because Carl didn't care for them too much.

It was an education, and I took it to heart. No, the recipe for the dough was not shared, but I still felt privileged to be able to see how the pies were created.

You know, there are no perfect families. Feuds happen, and a new feud opened up very quickly. Carl decided to open his own place over in Casscoe, which if you've been to Casscoe you know there's not much out there. He decided to start a diner behind his house, and for a little while he had some decent business. I even ate the first hamburger he ever sold. He made beignets, too, and the fried pies. He did that Monday through Friday, and then he'd head to DeValls Bluff and roll dough to get Viv through the morning on Saturday. Except he got uppity, and one day he told Viv he wasn't coming to do the pies that Saturday. Well, it didn't take long for friction to kick up, and when the dust settled, Carl's place had closed and Viv was only selling traditional pies, whole and by the slice.

More was to come. Viv's husband, Jess, had a health scare of some serious note, and Viv's granddaughter Addysynne had a wad of problems from the get-go, and life was so busy and complicated. The pie shop was quiet for a while.

That didn't stop Viv. Once Jess got better and Addy started growing like a weed, she went back to the shop and started selling her pies again, and some cakes too. And one day she stuck a status update on Facebook and asked if anyone wanted her to make fried pies again.

Oh man, the folks came outta the woodwork. Everywhere. They responded and begged and pleaded for Viv to bring back the pies. But how?

The secret was in the next generation. Viv's daughter Kim came in and started rolling that dough. And sure enough, they were just as good as ever before. I stood in the little vestibule of the pie shop on one hot August day in 2012 with my daughter and my photographer and tasted that same beautiful goodness—the crispy thin crust, the smooth as silk chocolate filling, the fresh strawberry pie with chunks of fresh berry still naturally sweet. My daughter ate most of mine. Viv filled us up with pie and Honeybun cake and introduced us to Addy and smiled and laughed.

Viv Barnhill and Addysynne at Ms. Lena's. *Grav Weldon.*

That day, that first day of the pies coming back, people came from all over. One of my old THV coworkers, Robert Settles, came out to pick up a box-worth. There were families that dropped by. There were Arkansawyers and folks from Tennessee and even a couple from New York who came through the door.

The fried pies that Lena Rice started making decades ago are still here, being made by her daughter and her granddaughter and one day by her great-great-granddaughter. They are splendid and they are memorable, and I have to give those little pies credit (along with their makers) for starting me off on the road that led me to this book.

If you go to Ms. Lena's, go on a Saturday or call Viv and let her know you'd like to come out and get some or get a pie or a cake beforehand. And if you decide to take pies home with you and notice they're not quite so crisp when you arrive at your destination, just put them in the fridge uncovered a bit. They'll crisp back up. I have no idea how they manage that, but it's a fact.

One More Note About Fried Pies

Don't let me mislead you. Fried pies may be the language of dough-wrapped pastry most prominent in the Delta, but they're not exclusive to the flatlands of eastern Arkansas. In fact, one of the best places to get a hand pie for the road is along U.S. 65 in Searcy County, on the northern edge of a tiny village called Leslie. That's where you'll find Misty's.

Opened in 1991, the convenience store quickly became a mainstay for locals, a place to chew the fat over biscuits in the morning and fried food all day and the only place in town you could get gas. Sharon Lewis bought the place in 1996 and has held onto it ever since, with a cadre of young (and young-at-heart) women who work behind the counter.

She also makes some marvelous fried pies. Every morning—and I do mean every morning, save perhaps Christmas—she starts cooking at 5:00 a.m. and sets in a supply of pies for the day. Each flour ball is rolled out into a six-inch diameter round, filled and finger-pressed. Each pie is fried, and the ones that aren't scooped up by early morning customers get wrapped in Saran wrap and stacked on the counter.

They come in so many flavors—the customary ones such as apple and chocolate, the less familiar types such as pecan and raisin and even rarer flavors like pineapple. She even does some sugar-free fillings in those salty-crusted pies. They're the perfect trucker food, and you'll see travelers pick one up along with a cola and a Ratchford Farms elk stick.

Fried pies
wrapped and
ready to go at
Misty's Shell
Station in Leslie.
Grav Weldon.

* * * * *

In so many places, including Feltner's Whatta-Burger in Russellville, the
Morrilton Drive-Inn Restaurant and four or five dozen other locations, you'll
find a simple fried pie that comes in a printed sleeve. These pies come from
Fly Wheel Pies in Prescott. They come in all sorts of flavors—blackberry,
sweet potato, chocolate and even sugar-free. Gary and Nell Ray "Fly Wheel"
Allen started the company back in 1984 in the Laneburg community. They
eventually moved into a shop on U.S. 67 in town. After Nell Ray died, Gary
remarried, and Rosemary Allen joined the business.

With the help of nine hired girls, the Allens put out enough pies to supply
dozens of restaurants, gas stations and country stores all across Arkansas.
In 2011, the place burned, and the then seventy-three-year-old Allen wasn't
sure if he was going to reopen or not. Demand being what it was, it wasn't
a month later that fried pies were coming back out of a temporary location.
So if you get a fried pie somewhere in Arkansas and your dining host tells
you they're Arkansas-made but not made in-house, chances are you've got
yourself a Fly Wheel pie.

* * * * *

Unless you don't. See, fried pies are so popular in Arkansas that there's a high demand. If you've gone somewhere in northwest Arkansas or someplace close by and you get a fried pie, it just might be a Letha's Fried Pie. That's Tim and Rhonda Glenn's place up in West Fork, and it's the second Letha's. The first one was run by Tim's parents, Tommy and Letha Glenn, first in Fayetteville and later out of Branson, Missouri. It was a traditional bakery, and like most places of the sort, it was full of love. But in 2009, the elder Glenns lost the bakery to fire. Everything was gone.

Rhonda Glenn wouldn't let it go. It didn't take long for her and Tim to regroup and come up with another idea—re-create Letha's in West Fork but as a wholesaler of fried pies.

It must have worked. Today, the Glenns and their staff churn out up to 1,200 pies a day, and they send them all over the place. I've encountered them here and there and at the Arkansas State Fair. My most recent experience was with their pecan fried pie at a little place called Grandpa's Barbeque up north of Cabot on Highway 367. The molten pie took a few minutes to fry up, but what I got was nothing short of wanton righteousness—pecans packed so tight there was barely room for the custard between, all hot and sweet and rich. The Glenns know what they're doing. They also make a dozen other flavors, and they ship them two dozen to a box all over the place.

One of Letha's Fried Pies at Grandpa's Bar-B-Que in Cabot. *Grav Weldon*.

Peanut butter pie at Godsey's Grill in Jonesboro. *Grav Weldon*.

Jonesboro, a City's Identity Through Pie

Jonesboro has its own sweet secrets.

Welcome to Jonesboro

The largest city in the Arkansas Delta holds a soft spot in my pie-seeking heart.

Back in the late 1990s, I spent three years in Jonesboro. I had gone to work for KAIT-TV, working my first full-time job as a television producer. It was also the second time I had moved away from Little Rock (the first being my move to Russellville to go to Arkansas Tech).

Jonesboro and that entire section of northeast Arkansas feels like a whole 'nother country from the rest of Arkansas. There's a different attitude, a slightly different accent and some very different political positions. Region Eight (the name still sticks) at the time was still a world away from Little Rock; you couldn't get to Jonesboro from anywhere outside the area on an interstate or a four-lane road.

My time there was an exciting one for Jonesboro. The city was expanding outside its insular ways and starting to grow. When I arrived in November 1995, there were few developments in the downtown area and not a lot of places to get alcohol. If you wanted liquor, you had to drive to Harrisburg, Weiner or Paragould or get a membership at the 501—not that I was ever much into that scene.

I was there for good times, like election days and the arrival of several big employers. I was there for the darkest times, too—especially the shootings at Westside Middle School in March 1998 and the Manila tornado a month later. I learned a lot about writing and news and human nature.

And I learned a lot about restaurants. My boyfriend at the time liked to go to a different restaurant any chance we got, and we managed to go to almost every restaurant in town. Jonesboro was saturated with good places to eat, particularly Chinese restaurants (more than a dozen), drive-ins, home cooking joints and Mexican restaurants. And, of course, Lazzari Italian Kitchen, the first place I ever dined in Jonesboro and the one place I have to go on every visit.

I left Jonesboro in the fall of 1998 and only visited once between 2000 and 2010, when I returned for a breakfast cover story I was working on for the *Arkansas Times*. Lazzari's is still there, along with Presley's Drive-In, the Front Page Café and Dragon City. But there are a lot of newcomers there too. And when I returned repeatedly to research pie, I discovered most of the best new pies came from these eateries, these upstarts that have blossomed in the largest city in Arkansas's Delta.

* * * * *

Sue's Kitchen closed in 1994, a year before I came to the city the first time. It had been the star of downtown eating, situated in the Church Street Station building. It was the heart's work of Sue Robinson Williams, who had been catering in the area since 1967. Williams started the restaurant in 1985 and had stayed with it for nearly a decade before turning the business back into a catering affair with Expressly Sue's Catering. She and her son John ran the catering business until 2005. He took a few restaurant management jobs here and then in the interim.

In August 2010, John Williams decided to reopen the restaurant in his mother's name, which definitely made her proud. And it's still there, a grand and beautiful jewel in a building that has served as a post office, a courthouse annex and a jail over its lifespan.

The cavernous main floor of the building is mostly open, with dainty tables and large windows. The menu is very much teahouse meets burger joint, with a nice selection of sandwiches, specials and salads. And on Saturday, there's a brunch.

And then there are the pies. Big refrigerator cases up front showcase great icebox and traditional pies, including the famed peanut butter pie for which Vincent Price once begged the recipe (yes, *that* Vincent Price) and a luscious pinker-than-pink delight called pink lemonade pie. A variation on the lemon icebox, this sweet-tart delicacy is uniformly a deep blush pink, drizzled with raspberry coulis and served with fresh unsweetened cream atop a thin graham cracker crust. It is the sort of pie you'd love to see at a cotillion or a little girl's tea party, delicate yet substantial and so tasty.

Pink lemonade pie at Sue's Kitchen in Jonesboro. *Grav Weldon.*

When you go to Sue's, you have to go during the lunch hour; it's only open for lunch Monday through Friday and Saturday for brunch. Check out the classy restored restrooms, and don't be afraid to ask for a window seat.

* * * * *

Skinny J's is just a few blocks over and up from Sue's Kitchen, but you might as well be walking a mile—there's at least a mile's difference between the two. While Sue's Kitchen is refined and elegant, Skinny J's is very denim and leather, woodsy and eclectic. It's American pub dining at its grooviest.

But besides the extensive list of appetizers, the burgers and nachos and other pub fare, you can order a house-made fried pie. The flavors are various, but the pecan fried pie is what you want. It's buttery and served hot, packed with little chunks of nuts and very flaky. It's also acceptable to eat two or three, since they're rather small (and inexpensive). However, if you order yours without ice cream, the management will want an explanation.

* * * * *

Cattycorner across Main Street you'll find Godsey's Grill, the trendiest, hippest joint in town. Godsey's is so hip, it's almost tragic, from the faux façade of replicated cola murals to the diagonal flooring (the rear of the place is set on an incline). It's the place to catch bands coming through town while knoshing on pizzas and flatbread sandwiches baked in a wood-fired oven.

It's also become known for its icebox pies, particularly a peanut butter version that's nutty and smooth. Godsey's makes the pie in-house, and it carries well, not being too sweet or too cloying. Pressed into a chocolate cookie crust and drizzled with chocolate, it's strangely filling. Share it with a hipster you love.

* * * * *

If you wander a mere half a block off Main Street, you'll step back a couple of generations. Chef's In is still the same sort of Boomer-friendly family buffet it has been for the past decade, and it's still serving the same sort of food—meatloaf, beef tips, liver and onions, fried chicken, fried catfish—you'd expect from a restaurant that had been around half a century.

Breakfast is served each weekday, and then there's lunch, which is served for one price including the entrée, sides, dessert and beverage. I've been warned I would fall in love with the banana pillows they serve, but I have never caught them. I have seen the chocolate cream pie and the pecan pie. But the pie most worthy of note is another heritage pie—a raisin pie. Layered on top of a pastry crust, the blend of vanilla custard speckled with raisins is something I've only ever seen at a family gathering. The custard is prepared hot and the raisins dropped in, which causes them to expand and rehydrate. The result is a pie that has that great raisin-vanilla flavor throughout, with almost chunky raisins from the process.

* * * * *

The one place I loved most for pie during my KAIT years was a joint called Ann's Restaurant. It was a great little lunchroom in Fountain Square, and it served up a great meat-and-three every day.

Ann's is gone…and it's not. It started up in the 1980s, had a long run and then switched names in 2011. Today it's called Gina's Place, and it still serves up great counter-service food amidst a family photo–strewn lunchroom, by members of the same family. Every day there are three entrées to choose from and well over a dozen side items. The same cold plate featuring your choice of four items (including creamy pimento cheese, chicken salad, tuna salad, potato salad, green bean salad, red bean salad, orange Jell-O salad, tossed salad, coleslaw, cottage cheese or peaches) is still offered, and there are still pies on the menu. Just about any day you can get pecan, chocolate cream, coconut cream or Key lime.

And then there's the peanut butter pie. It's one of the richest peanut butter pies I have found anywhere, served up on a homemade crust made from peanut butter sandwich cookies, filled with mousse-like peanut butter custard and topped with whipped cream, peanuts and chocolate chips. It's a meal in a pie, with all that filling peanut butter within. It's not too thick, but it is quite fluffy, and somehow it just kills the appetite.

Lemon icebox pie slices at the Skillet Restaurant at the Ozark Folk Center in Mountain View. *Kat Robinson*.

PART VI

Signature Pies of Arkansas

Even more marvelous pies found throughout the state

Pecan Pie at
Your Mama's Good Food

Ah, the pecan pie. Or Karo-nut pie. Or whatever you like to call it. We as southerners teeth on pecan pie. The depths of a good pecan suspension and the flavors of crust versus nuts are things that attenuate us toward who we are and what we will become. I do believe there's a good part of pecan in most Arkansawyers (those with allergies set aside, of course).

Pecan pie at Your Mama's Good Food in Little Rock. *Kat Robinson.*

To find a decent one is not hard; there's a pretty standard recipe that most folks follow. To find a good one isn't too challenging. To find a spectacular, unadulterated pie though? That's a rare thing. So to find one in the most mundane of lunchtime spots in the middle of downtown Little Rock is heartening.

At Your Mama's Good Food on Second Street, good home cooking is the norm. Whether it's fried chicken, chicken fried steak, meatloaf or roast beef, the restaurant's the place to go and get some vittles and sides for lunch. The rolls are huge and pliant, and there is always a choice of pies and cobbler for dessert. And the pecan pie is the best one of the bunch.

Unlike so many pecans-on-the-top custard-rich pies, Your Mama's Good Food packs them in tight. There are tiny bits of nut throughout, suspended in the Karo-nut custard and packed in the surface, a single half on top to illustrate just what sort of nut was dismembered for this pie project. The syrup soaks into the crust for a delicious homogeny of flavor, all nut and syrup and a little salt in the sweetness, a sop-up-syrup in the morning sort of flavor, a hint of what might be maple flavoring, a touch of vanilla.

The texture is the thing, though. Instead of a pasty custard or a runny one, or even a gelatinous one, every single bite has those crushed pecans in it.

Chess Pie at Alley Oops

James Beard will tell you all about what's in a chess pie. Well, maybe he won't anymore, but he woulda, and he did in his 1972 book *American Cookery*. The book describes the pie as being made from eggs, butter, sugar, vanilla and cornmeal. But there's also the matter of that name.

You can find chess pie here in Arkansas. There are several places that happen to sell it, foremost among them Alley-Oops in Little Rock. It's also a favorite with home cooks in rural areas, especially for putting together a last-minute dish.

But what a funny name, "chess" pie. The significance? Some speculate it comes from the southern way of speaking. Just as words like "aight" (pronounced "ite") are common in speech in some areas (particularly northeast Arkansas), the term "chess" was likely another interpretation of someone's drawl. I suspect someone with a little more proper book learning asked one of these home chefs, "What sort of pie is that?" and was answered, "Just pie." Sound it out.

If you want the chess pie at Alley Oops, you call before you go. Chef Gary Duke only makes up a certain number each day, and when they're gone, you're out of luck. Alley Oops has been around for a quarter of a century now. It was located at Kanis and Shackleford Road before there was much past either one out in West Little Rock. About a dozen years ago, the folks who ran it picked up and moved a half mile to the west. Today, the little quaint American restaurant with the feel of a sports bar sits on the end of a plaza at Kanis and Bowman.

Chess pie at Alley Oops in Little Rock. *Kat Robinson.*

You go to Alley Oops for a good reasonably priced lunch in between shifts, especially if you're working at Baptist Health Medical Center or one of the local medical clinics that line Kanis Road to the east. You get a po'boy or a big plate of nachos, but when you order, you get your pie.

Duke always makes chess pie, and he usually makes chocolate chess pie as well. The two are similar in appearance, except one is yellow and one is brown. The yellow one is just about perfect, just the right amount of sweetness to make everything fine. The chocolate chess pie, though— well, it's marvelous in its own right, the missing link between chess pie and brownies with that thin crisp top crust good brownies form. And some days there are other variations, like Almond Joy.

I can't make a chess pie as well as Gary Duke does. But I can sure take a stab at it.

Chocolate chess pie at Alley Oops in Little Rock. *Kat Robinson.*

Chocolate Chess Pie

1½ cups sugar

3 tablespoons cocoa

3 beaten eggs

5 tablespoons evaporated milk

2 teaspoons apple cider vinegar

1 tablespoon vanilla extract

4 tablespoons melted butter

1 flour-and-butter blind-baked pie crust

Sift together sugar and cocoa. Beat together eggs, milk, vinegar, vanilla and butter. Add sugar and cocoa and incorporate. Pour into pie crust and bake at 350° for 35 minutes or until surface begins to form bubbly pits and is firm.

Buttermilk Pie at O'Henry's

Most buttermilk pies I've encountered tend to be creamy or mild. There's one, though, that defies that norm—and that's at O'Henry's outside Conway.

The bright yellow wedge is extraordinarily light and extraordinarily tart, with a definite flavor of lemon and buttermilk throughout. There's a nice

Buttermilk pie at O'Henry's near Conway. *Kat Robinson.*

buttery flavor to it as well, a touch of caramelization to the impossibly well-fluffed pie. I'm not used to that strength of flavor in a buttermilk pie. I'm used to the nice toasty flavor of the crust and the creamy bits inside. This one? Just one layer after another of tart. Heavenly tart, at that. Yes, I'll order it again next time.

There are other pies on the menu as well—pecan, chocolate cream, coconut cream and apple, as well as cheesecake and ice cream.

You'll find O'Henry's on Highway 365 parallel to I-40. To get there, take the Mayflower exit, go a block west and turn right; it'll be on the right. Or take Harkrider from Dave Ward in Conway; it's a couple miles south on the left.

Chocolate and Peanut Butter Meringue Pie at Martha Jean's Diner

If you head north out of Beebe on Highway 367, if you watch for it and don't overshoot it, you can find a gray building set back from the road a bit. This is Martha Jean's Diner, and it is the unheralded spot for a good bite around those parts.

Open for most every meal except Sunday dinner, the place serves up what you'd come to expect with good country cooking. And there are always pies—not just the traditional favorites but splendid renditions of German chocolate, blackberry cream cheese and something that should be considered the epitome of the deadly sin of gluttony. Of course, I am talking about the restaurant's thick, fudge-like chocolate peanut butter meringue pie. Not only does Martha Jean's serve up one of the strongest, thickest custards ever discovered for a chocolate pie, not only does the place smash it down on a thick layer of peanut butter cream—but the whole mess is topped with a lofty, impossible meringue. I dare you to eat a whole slice yourself. Oh, you did? You naughty, naughty diner.

Motorcycle Delights at Oark General Store and Catalpa General Store

There are several restaurants across the state that claim to be the oldest. Oark has a really good claim. While Franke's Cafeteria in Little Rock can prove it has continuously operated since 1919, the Oark General Store can point out it was established in 1890. While the store has been in continuous operation, the restaurant within has been there some years and not some others since its inception. The place is a classic and worthy of a dash off I-40.

It's a ways up and away from things. You can get there a number of ways, but they're each going to be long. Adventurers go up 103 from Clarksville and wind all through the Ozarks. You can also get there by the Pig Trail, Highway 23. Either way, you head north from I-40 to Highway 215 and head west—some of the best motorcycling country in the state.

You know you're in for good pie when you come in and hear the slogan "Walk In, Waddle Out." The Oark General Store makes up plate lunches every day, breakfast every morning and what's rumored to be the best burger in the Ozarks. The surroundings are quaint, the conversation is lively and the iced tea keeps coming. The General Store to this day sells camping gear, provisions and whatnots. It's a living museum.

The pies? They are old-fashioned, and there's nothing wrong with that. The peach pie I had from the store was country heaven: recently picked and sliced peaches in spices and sugar, nestled between a top and bottom crust both buttery and salty. This is an ice cream–worthy pie. The pecan pie is also a decadent treat.

Top: Oark General Store. *Grav Weldon*.

Above: Catalpa General Store. *Grav Weldon*.

Opposite, top: Oark General Store. *Grav Weldon*.

Opposite, bottom: Peach pie at Oark General Store. *Grav Weldon*.

If the pie at Oark wasn't hard enough to get to, you're in luck. One of the prettiest drives in all of Arkansas starts at Oark and goes due east on Highway 215 to a tiny little spot on the road right near where it turns to gravel. That's where you'll find the Catalpa General Store. Out in the middle of nowhere, this place is getting rave reviews from motorcyclists who seek out curvy routes through the area.

Plate lunches are the thing at Catalpa, and most of the vegetables that end up on your plate come from a little garden plot across the road. And then there are the pies—big generous pies made the old-fashioned way. Fruit pies have lattice tops, custard pies are topped with meringue and all of them are divine. The lemon meringue is the mildest I've encountered in the state, a cool and creamy opaque yellow curd topped with a mildly toasted top. The apple pie is richly spiced and buttery, while the butterscotch pie is powerful and deep.

Coconut Meringue Pie at 65ᵗʰ Street Diner

Let's hear it for the working class. That's most of us, right? 65ᵗʰ Street Diner is the sort of place where the blue-collar sort congregate for a good meal and a sweet treat during the lunch hour. The sort of place where the colloquial Little Rock–style greeting of "Good to see ya!" is uttered back and forth, both as a greeting to passersby and by individuals wanting to cut short the conversation so they can dive into their dinner.

The folks who turn out at the diner are the sort of folks in your neighborhood—the local sheriff's deputy, the guy who works down at the cola plant, a couple of girls in accounting at the trucking company, that sort of thing. They come to the 65ᵗʰ Street Diner for a good hot meal to get them through the afternoon, with food like good fried chicken, stuffed bell peppers, peas, Brussels sprouts, glazed carrots, chicken and dumplings and all other sorts of good home cooking. And then they do pie, all sorts of it, all pre-wrapped in Saran wrap on a Styrofoam plate—lemon, cherry, pumpkin, pecan, chocolate, apple and coconut.

And what a coconut meringue, creamy to the point of almost running. Once that piece is pulled out of the refrigerator case, it's just a matter of time before the meringue slides glacially to rest on the side of the plate—that is, if you don't eat it first. It's more likely to run in the summertime, when the temperatures are bumping up against one hundred and the heat oozes through even the most polarized north-facing glazed window.

Best of all, the pies are cheap, aimed at the sort of guy or gal who wants to pick up a sweet to take with them back to work when they head on to the tire

Coconut meringue pie at 65th Street Diner in Little Rock. *Kat Robinson.*

bladder place, the air conditioner place or work at the Arkansas Foodbank or the Arkansas Rice Depot down the street. And when lunch is over, it's over, so you'd better clean your plate and make your exit before 2:00 p.m.

Key Lime Pie at Dave's Place

I'm all about a bargain, and maybe that's why I am keen on Dave's Place on Center Street in Little Rock. The long restaurant a block and a half from the Statehouse Convention Center is your usual soup-and-sandwich sort of place for downtown diners with little time to spare and no desire to move parked cars.

Of course, it could be too easy to shortchange the place based on that assessment. So don't. Instead, go if you can (there's metered parking out front) and grab yourself a good sandwich or one of the specials (listed each day on the eatery's website). And don't miss out on having dessert. Each day, there's something different. I rather enjoyed this memory-evoking slice of Key lime pie. No, it wasn't some fruit-bit-laden entity of out-of-state procurement, nor was it some creation that came packaged in a box from the freezer case. This was one of those southern granny specials where Key lime juice meets sweetened condensed milk, and it made me very, very happy. Can't beat the price either—just a buck.

Key lime pie at Dave's Place in Little Rock. *Kat Robinson.*

Coconut Meringue Pie at Lewis Family Restaurant

There's nothing like a good made-from-scratch meal. Lewis Family Restaurant has been making just that sort of food since 1993. The flat-topped building at Zero and U.S. 71 B in Fort Smith serves up fresh-made pancakes, omelets and bacon at breakfast and plate lunches with southern favorites—and a burger that's considered to be so spicy you'd be a fool to consume it. Actually, if you manage to eat the Inferno Burger—

Coconut meringue pie at Lewis' Family Restaurant in Fort Smith. *Grav Weldon.*

seasoned beef topped with spicy bacon, pepper jack cheese, jalapeños and onions on a bun smothered in Lewis's own *hot* chipotle mayo—you gain entrance to a very exclusive club of folks who have a special table at the restaurant.

The pies served up are what you expect for a family restaurant—pecan, coconut, chocolate, apple, cherry. The egg custard is the best in the city, hands down, don't you argue with me none.

But I also love the coconut meringue, and for good reason. The meringue is light and sweet with so much coconut in it I'm not sure how it could stand. The custard is creamy and rich, with visible shreds of coconut throughout, a nice blind-baked pastry, crumbly in all the right places. The custard has a flavor to it reminiscent of maple syrup but stronger even with the flavor of honey, and maybe even a little salt. The meringue clings to the custard sweetly and securely throughout consumption. What a pie.

Lemon Icebox Pie at Rita's

When I was in college, my boyfriend and I often took to the roads around Russellville and just drove around when we had free time. A summertime drive brought us to Hector, where we found Rita's Restaurant. The year: 1993. The temperature: well above ninety. We were hot, we were thirsty and we needed a bite to eat.

I do recall at the time how pleased we were with the air conditioning, the sloppy wet roast beef sandwich we shared and the waitress who never let our glasses get past half empty. And I remember a certain strawberry icebox pie that was just delightful.

Nearly two decades passed before I darkened that door again. Working on assignment for *Arkansas Wild* one February day in 2011, my photographer and I decided to take the scenic route up to Marshall and passed through Hector on a Sunday morning. And there it was, Rita's Restaurant (since 1989), on the south side of town, west side of the road. Of course, I had somewhere I needed to be, so we didn't stop.

Yet that afternoon coming back, I kept thinking about Rita's and wondered if it would be anything like what it had been. Already having eaten, I wasn't hungry for a big meal, but passing through the communities of Welcome Home, Tilly and Nogo, I had that familiar sensation. I had a hankering for pie. So once we were back in the big-time city limits of Hector (population 534), we headed to Rita's for some iced tea and whatever pie they had on hand.

When we walked in, one of the ladies behind the counter told us to sit where we liked. She asked if we'd been there before. When I told her it'd been more

Lemon icebox pie at Rita's in Hector. *Grav Weldon.*

than a decade and a half, she mentioned that the folks running the place now had taken it over a few months earlier. That was a slight cause for concern.

I needn't have worried. With the exception of an added Pizza Pro menu, it had barely changed—a variety of sandwiches, burgers, home cooking and such. And the desserts were still listed on a whiteboard at the front. The day's options included lemon iced box (their spelling), coconut cream, cheesecake and peach and apple fried pies. I wanted and needed some pie, and the iced box pie sounded good. So that's what was ordered, along with some fried mushrooms to balance out the sweet.

The pie came to us first, an ample tall slice of homogenous whipped pie. It didn't look like a whole lot, I will give you that, sorta yellow but more beige on a tan crust. I felt differently when I tasted it, though.

Unlike the error so many places make when dealing with lemon, this was neither overly sweet nor overly tart. It was a simple blend of lemon zest, cream cheese and perhaps sour cream, sugar and whatever other goodness was in there, all piled into a crushed vanilla wafer crust. It was light and it was mild, not very sweet or tangy but substantial in its flavor-weight, cleansing the palate. Refreshing, simple, beautiful.

I had to set down my fork and look at it. It was so humble but so good. The flavor didn't leave me when I'd stopped; it just stayed there on my tongue and hinted at lemon a little longer. Not too cloying, just there.

The fried mushrooms were good and plentiful enough, cooked golden brown and served with ranch dressing. They were great to share, too. But I still kept looking at that pie and had to go back to finish it off.

There was nothing over-the-top about it. No sprinkles, no whipped cream, it wasn't a la mode or set aflame or anything else. Now, why can't more places serve up pie like that these days? This is Sunday potluck dinner pie. This is the sort of pie people bring to spring picnics. I want some more.

Of course, there's no guarantee that pie will be there when I get back. All pies at Rita's Restaurant are made fresh each morning, and when they're out they're out. If they sell them all before you get there, you can console yourself with a milkshake. Find Rita's Restaurant on Highway 27 in Hector.

Grasshopper Pie at Club 178

Great restaurants make stuff from scratch. Club 178 in Bull Shoals makes its sauces, its dressings, its pastries, its rubs and a whole host of other things from scratch, including an ever-changing array of desserts.

The club itself is an interesting building. It's an upscale restaurant attached to, of all things, a bowling alley. I was told when I asked about the unusual juxtaposition that the bowling alley was a labor of love, that the restaurant owners' son was a budding bowler and that the alley was built so he'd have a place to strike pins.

Among the delicacies offered at Club 178 was this grasshopper pie. The mint-and-chocolate pie was very popular in the family circles I traveled in as a child. But I have seen that combination very little in restaurants as an adult. Oh, sure, you can get mint chocolate chip ice cream at the store. There's even a gum that's mint chocolate chip, which I find a little strange. I've had mint leaves atop different chocolate confections by our local top-shelf chefs, but this one simple pie has not been on any menu I've nodded my way through in quite a while. The closest I've seen has been the mint chocolate chip ice cream pie at Hunka Pie, and while it's on the menu, I can't recall actually seeing it offered on any visit I've been there.

So hearing grasshopper pie mentioned by our waitress in her spiel was ear catching. And yes, it was green. Grasshopper pie *should* be green. Additionally, it was not a Jell-O pie or an ice cream pie. This was a marshmallow-based pie. I could taste the crème de menthe (where the green came from) clearly but not too strongly, just enough to balance out against the Oreo

Club 178 in Bull Shoals. *Grav Weldon*.

Grasshopper pie at Club 178. *Grav Weldon*.

cookie crust. There was also a light chocolaty taste, probably from crème de cacao. It was served up with a drizzle of good old-fashioned Hershey syrup (like the stuff from the can, remember that?), slightly chilled with some whipped cream to boot. It was, in many ways, just minty enough to negate the need for an after-dinner mint.

Club 178 is a rather neat place. Reservations are suggested, though not required, and it's casual. Try it when you're in Bull Shoals.

Chocolate Meringue Pie at the Country Rooster

B etween the walls of the Country Rooster in Green Forest, you'll find all sorts of things: beautiful glassware in almost every color of the rainbow, records from ages and ages of vinyl, canned goods of various sorts, books, memorabilia, furniture—and pie.

The store on the town square also serves as a lunchroom that has earned a golden reputation. I've been told about the legendary lasagna and the meatloaf, said to be some of the best in the county. Lunches, desserts and everything else are served on dinnerware appropriate for the situation— reclaimed plates with mismatched silverware. The chocolate meringue pie I sought out on my visit was served on a tray likely older than I was, an old square metal TV tray delivered to one of the many different dining tables in the middle of the store. The custard was very firm and thick, and the meringue had a nice browning to it. The meringue was pleasant and not too sweet. The chocolate custard was nicely rich, almost pudding-like. It was a decent slice of pie.

You'll find the Country Rooster on the square in Green Forest, right on U.S. 62.

Snickers Pie at Neighbor's Mill

The building looks like it has been in place forever, as if the world has grown up around it. But Neighbor's Mill has only been standing since 1999 on U.S. 65 on the north side of Harrison.

Inspired by the one-hundred-plus-year-old gristmill they still use to grind the whole grain to make the rich flour for their breads and pastries, Mike and Karin Nabors created this oasis that serves a community and a broadening band of tourists who travel the highway into and out of Arkansas. Within the old brick walls are a bakery, a great kitchen for picking up breakfast or lunch, spacious dining in an airy environment and perhaps the cleanest and most comfortable restrooms between Little Rock and Branson.

Neighbor's is known for a lot of things. The bread is popular and fresh made every day, with variations like the multi-grain Woodstock and the rich Four Cheese and Rotel always popular and available. Soups are good, as are the sandwiches, and there is always a plethora of options ranging from sweet fruit breads to the much ballyhooed pumpkin cream cheese muffins.

Neighbor's also excels with pastries, and every day there's a selection of pie slices offered, some perched atop the counter on ceramic plates with a tent of plastic wrap, some ensconced in a highlighted display case, drizzled with sauce or caramel. Among their best sweet offerings: a Snickers pie, with its nougat-like cream cheese layer, with caramel and a smooth cap of chocolate ganache. Rich and thick, it captures the flavors of the popular candy bar and accurately translates them into this chilled delight.

Top: Neighbor's Mill in Harrison. *Grav Weldon*.

Left: Snickers pie at Neighbor's Mill. *Grav Weldon*.

Pineapple Delight at the Red Oak Fillin' Station

There are some pies that work much better in the summer and others that work much better in the winter. Pumpkin and sweet potato pies tend to be wintery pies, as are pecan pies. Icebox and cream pies and fresh fruit pies are summer-friendly.

You can't get much more summer-friendly than the Pineapple Delight pie at the Red Oak Fillin' Station outside Hot Springs. This last-stop convenience-store-slash-gas-station-slash-restaurant serves up a selection of different pies every day, along with home-cooking specials and burgers.

Like most convenience stores, it has a couple pumps out front, and you can pick up drinks and motor oil and Little Debbie snack cakes inside. But you know it's different when you walk through the door. There are several mismatched dining room tables and chairs set up around the south side of the room, short bar stools at a wall counter and a menu. And sit-down service, as in if you aren't about to leave you'd better sit.

The pies offered each day are kept in a big pie case in the counter, right next to the call window from the kitchen. These aren't hoity-toity pies. They're just about what you'd get if you went and found a maternal relative of a certain age who was preparing something sweet for Sunday potluck. For instance, the Key lime pie sitting in the case is akin to the old Eagle Brand Condensed Milk recipe version. They also make a mean baked peach pie.

And then there's the Pineapple Delight. Think ambrosia—not necessarily the nectar of the gods but the sort of stuff you get at those Sunday picnics, which includes marshmallow fluff and coconut flakes and bits of fruit. Big fluffy creamy marshmallow-infused goodness coagulated together with coconut flakes and lots of juicy bits of shredded pineapple, straight from the can and into a pressed graham crust. It is fluffy and cold and slightly tart and sweet without being cloying. Another lick-the-plate sort of pie.

You'll find the Red Oak Fillin' Station at 2169 Carpenter Dam Road on the southeast side of Hot Springs, on the way out to Garvan Woodland Gardens.

Coconut Cream Pie at the Skillet Restaurant and Ozark Fried Pies at the Smokehouse

Arkansas is blessed with geographic diversity, with a Delta plain that stretches to the edge of the sky, with the rolling Ouachita Mountains, with the eroded plateaus of the Ozarks and with the heavily forested timberlands of the South. In every section of the state, you'll find state parks where you can enjoy the beauty of these amazing surroundings.

I know; you may be expecting a bit of a sales pitch, and in the interest of full disclosure I must point out once again that at the time of this writing I am the communications manager for the Arkansas Department of Parks and Tourism. That's a development that came late into my pie search but one for which I feel particularly blessed.

That doesn't really have any influence over what I do food-wise. And I can honestly say, the Skillet Restaurant at the Ozark Folk Center in Mountain View happens to have not only some of the best fried chicken in the state but great pies as well.

The Skillet serves both the park and the community seven days a week during the park's season. Breakfast is a buffet that includes egg casserole, sausage and bacon, big biscuits and grits and the like. Lunch and dinner during the week are an off-the-menu event, but on Sunday there's that fried chicken and home-style vegetables and whatnot. All good.

Among the offerings Ms. Nina puts out are pies, decadent and rich and wonderful pies. They're put out on a table, and you better get what you want quick else it run out. The coconut cream is especially good, with coconut whipped both into the custard below and the cream on top. She does a

Chocolate peanut butter pie at the Skillet Restaurant at the Ozark Folk Center in Mountain View. *Kat Robinson.*

Fried pies at the Smokehouse at the Ozark Folk Center in Mountain View. *Kat Robinson.*

mean chocolate peanut butter pie too, drizzled with more peanut butter and chocolate on top, a splendid choice.

One more hint. If you've already driven to Mountain View, it would behoove you to enjoy the Ozark Folk Center and all its resident craftsmen, artisans and performers. It would also be a good bet to drop in on the Smokehouse inside the park. Yes, you'll find great smoked meats there. But you'll also find fried pies. These biscuit-crusted fruit-filled hand pies are the perfect snack for taking with you as you visit with the craftsmen and observe the demonstrations offered at this popular Arkansas state park.

Ozark Folk Center Fried Pie

3 ounces evaporated milk

½ cup water

½ cup block shortening (a stick of Crisco), melted

1 ounce white vinegar

2 cups self-rising flour

½ cup plain flour

8 ounces of filling (this can be chocolate custard, a cooked fruit mélange, etc.)

Mix together evaporated milk, water, shortening and white vinegar. Blend flour into liquid. Using an electric mixer, mix until texture of dough is silky, not sticky or dry. Adjust with small amounts of liquid if too dry to roll or small amount of flour if sticky.

Pull an amount the size of a big walnut and roll into ball. Roll into a six-inch circle on floured board or parchment paper.

Place four ounces of any type of filling toward one side of the circle. Brush the edges of the circle with evaporated milk. Fold in half and seal edges with fork or fingers. Punch holes in the top using a fork two times. This prevents explosion.

Use vegetable oil to deep fry at temperature of 350° for 5 minutes or until golden brown. If you pan fry, turn pies when first side browns. Makes a dozen.

Lemon Icebox Pie at Mather Lodge

Petit Jean State Park is the oldest park in the Arkansas State Park system—but the restaurant? Well, there's been a restaurant at Mather Lodge at the park as long as I can remember. The food was always pretty decent, but the décor? You could take or leave it.

Lemon icebox pie at Mather Lodge at Petit Jean State Park near Morrilton. *Kat Robinson.*

Until now. In May 2011, the newly renovated Mather Lodge opened. Architects were careful to include the original lodge reception areas in its construction, but they took off the 1970s addition and replaced it with a carefully conceived lodge-style dining room and state-of-the-art kitchen. The new facility looks like it's been there for generations.

What pie should you eat at Mather Lodge? Why, the lemon icebox, of course. Tart and sweet and very strong, it's a sharing pie, the sort of pie you'll want coffee with. And you can even make it at home.

Mather Lodge's Lemon Icebox Pie

1 16-ounce package frozen lemonade concentrate
2 16-ounce tubs whipped topping
2 14-ounce cans sweetened condensed milk
4 graham cracker crusts

Blend concentrate, whipped topping and condensed milk. Pour into pie crust. Chill for one hour. Top with graham cracker crumbs and/or whipped topping if you choose.

Sweet Potato Pie at Lindsey's Hospitality House

The best barbecue places serve up pie. And many of the best places for barbecue around here serve up sweet potato pie. Those notes tend to resonate well together.

Lindsey's Hospitality House in North Little Rock offers some of the best sweet potato pie in Arkansas, right alongside some unabashedly rugged 'cue. It's different from the really sweet and really tangy pies served around these parts. It's not especially sweet, almost meaty, a mouth-filling, strong-flavored pie that about whomps you upside the head with cinnamon, nutmeg, allspice and cloves, a real workingman's pie guaranteed to satisfy any remnants of an appetite left over from a good lunch.

Apple fried pie at Lindsey's Hospitality House in North Little Rock. *Kat Robinson.*

Better than that, Lindsey's serves up other pies too, including a daily rotating selection of fried pies and an egg custard that's the best in the city, no joke—creamy, smooth and with a crown top of nutmeg that will make you humble. The fried pies are perfect for purses but not pockets, big enough to end a meal yet small enough to not feel guilty about.

Bourbon Pecan Pie at Ralph's Pink Flamingo BBQ

Ralph's Pink Flamingo BBQ started off as something different. See, back in 1998, Ralph Taylor and Tim McGuire decided to do something crazy. They decided to go enter a barbecue competition in town over at Columbus Acres in Fort Smith—and what do you know, they won first place in pork.

Now some folks would have just taken their good fortune in stride and carried on as normal. Not these guys. They revved it up, learned all they could about barbecue and set out on the competition circuit. They joined the Kansas City BBQ Society and started attending those sanctioned events in 2001. They called themselves Pink Flamingo BBQ because, as they say, "we're cheap, we're tacky and you don't want us in your yard." In 2003, they won First Place Sausage at the American Royal competition (against nearly five hundred other competitors), which is why they always have a piece of sausage on the dinner plates they serve up.

Eventually, Ralph's wife and two sons joined the team, making it a family affair. And eventually the restaurant was opened on the corner of Old Greenwood and Country Club, in the corner of an L-shaped shopping center.

They love bright colors inside, as we discovered on our visit there. I wanted a substantial lunch along with my pie quest, but the first stop was to the pie case. Within was a plethora of chocolate-covered strawberries on plates, plated slices of strawberry cake—and slices of what appeared to be chocolate pecan pie.

You know I claimed that right off the bat.

Bourbon pecan pie at Ralph's Pink Flamingo BBQ in Fort Smith. *Grav Weldon*.

And you know what? This pie, this bourbon chocolate pecan pie, is a sin. It's probably the most alcoholic pie I have encountered on my trek. It tasted like the Pillsbury Doughboy had taken a shine to Jim Beam and had decked him one. Not that the flavors were drowned out by the bourbon, either; there were huge chocolate chunks in amidst the pecans and custard. It is a worthy pie and worth a sit-down at a good barbecue restaurant. I shall dine there again.

Banana Pudding Pie at the Backyard Bar-B-Que Company

By this point in the book, you should be assured of the natural relationship between good barbecue joints and pie. For some reason, pie is the natural finish to a dinner of pork butt, ribs or the like.

In Magnolia, if you want barbecue and pie, you go to the Backyard Bar-B-Que Company. It's a great local joint with a lot of good stuff to eat. I have

at one point sat in there and watched a woman half my size finish off an entire slab of ribs and a couple of sides and still go back for pie. It is that good; it's the sort of good you might injure yourself on.

The pie case at the Backyard Bar-B-Que Company in Magnolia. *Kat Robinson.*

Ms. Glenda makes all the pies, and she keeps the cooler full of delights such as pecan cream cheese, chocolate, coconut meringue and more. Folks swear by that pecan cream cheese, but I had to try something different whilst I was there, which is how I ended up with an impossible slice of banana pudding pie. No joke, the pie stomps hard on the line between pie and pudding. While yes, it's meringue on top and crust on the bottom, in between lies a thick vanilla custard with chunks of banana and vanilla wafers. It's tasty, hard to define and definitely an original.

Peanut Butter Pie at Three Sam's Barbeque Joint

Most people never get to the desserts at Three Sam's Barbeque Joint because the portions are large and tasty. But for those who have sampled them—well, you know what I am talking about.

The pie search took me to Mabelvale, out on the southwest fringe of the Little Rock metropolitan area, early one lunchtime while I was en route to another engagement. I knew I wouldn't have time to dine in, so I placed an order to go—one beef barbecue sandwich and one slice of the famed peanut butter pie.

Problem with this is that I had to wait—which, yes, I expected—but because I was waiting, I had to stand next to the counter and its sweet corner. Everything under glass there looked too good to pass up—the luscious Italian cream cake, the decadent brownies and especially the peanut butter cookies under their neat little dome. I could have eaten a dozen of them. Instead, I waited.

And when I received my repast in a bag to take with me, I took it out carefully and shot it in the parking lot, sitting in my vehicle and wishing I had time to eat it inside. See, Three Sam's *smells* fantastic. I coulda sat in there and enjoyed five senses' worth of amazing. But I had to run.

The beef sandwich was all over the place—chopped smoky beef under a pile of creamy slaw on a seedless bun. It was served up with a pickle, a package of Lay's and a container of the thinnish, savory, slightly tangy sauce

Peanut butter pie at Three Sam's in Mabelvale. *Kat Robinson*.

the place is known for. It's not a sweet sauce by any means, but it is smoky and soakable. And the meat completely doesn't need it. This is one case where the barbecue meat and the barbecue sauce are equally good.

But I hadn't come for the sandwich; that was a fringe benefit. I came for the pie. And the little box that contained the pie felt like it weighed a pound. Inside was the most peanut-y of peanut butter pies I had ever encountered. It was nearly two inches thick, topped with peanuts and chunks of peanut butter cups. The mousse-style filling was dense and a little salty in addition to being sweet.

The winner for me, though, was the sweet peanut buttery bottom crust—a crust likely made from flour, butter, peanut butter and peanuts but which tasted of those peanut butter sandwich cookies the Girl Scouts sell each year. There was not a part of this pie that had not been graced with the magic of peanut butter. Just might be the best peanut butter pie in all of central Arkansas.

You'll find Three Sam's Barbeque Joint next to the railroad tracks in downtown Mabelvale.

Key Lime Pie at Rolando's Restaurante

Rolando's is a Latin restaurant; it's not Mexican, not quite South American. The cuisine is exotic and popular, and if you get a chance to drop into one of the three locations around the state, you really do need to try the Quesadilla de Chivo—it's incredible.

Key lime pie at Rolando's Restaurante in Hot Springs. *Grav Weldon.*

It's not the sort of place you'd see pie on the menu, but it's there—a grand Key lime pie that's one of my favorites. I'm not much on thick-crust pies, but I'm able to overlook the overenthusiastic graham cracker crust with this one because the custard within is so good. Fresh key limes, very tart, make not just the traditional custard base but also the whipped layer above, giving two entirely different texture sensations. It's topped with generous dollops of whipped cream and a nice counterpoint drizzle of raspberry coulis that somehow isn't as tart as this pie.

Here's the thing. If you go to the Hot Springs location, there's this patio. If it's not one hundred degrees outside, it's a grand oasis away from Bathhouse Row and Central Avenue, and you should enjoy it. Sometimes there's live music. Always there's great food.

There are three locations, in Fort Smith, Rogers and Hot Springs. So there's really no excuse to miss the place.

Peanut Butter Meringue Pie at South End Grill

Batesville is home to many unique things. It's the hometown of NASCAR driver Mark Martin, who owns a car dealership on the south side of town that features a museum with his old race cars. It's home to Lyon College, a very respectable private university that celebrates each spring with a Scottish festival. And it's home to a peanut butter meringue pie.

The South End Grill really is on the south side of town, way out 167 on the other side of the airport. I dropped in one Wednesday evening with another of my many traveling companions, searching out sustenance before a weekend of getaway time. When we entered, I made a beeline for the counter, lured by the vision of three very toasty-looking meringue pies. They looked alien and unusual, tanned lumpy meringues that looked like the topography of some distant mountainous nation. They also smelled quite good.

My companion that night ordered up a twelve-ounce ribeye steak, and I chose what I thought would be a quick bite: the Open Face Beef Sandwich. Our waitress brought my companion a salad with two containers of red something, one of which, I believe, might have been ketchup. It was all right. It ate.

Our dinners were delivered, and we were just shocked. My companion's steak continued all the way across the plate—one side to the other—his fried squash and fried okra piled on top concealing about half of it. And my meal wasn't a sandwich; it was a hot mess that took up the entire platter. All good, but too much to consume at once with any hope at acquiring and tasting some pie.

I had been told about peanut butter pie but had only seen meringue offered. Turns out, yes, the peanut butter pie *was* a meringue pie. When my slice arrived, I carefully scoped it out. Eschewing thick or mousse-like textures like normal peanut butter pie, this was a nice light egg custard–type pie, very moist under the meringue. The meringue itself was so toasty that the top bit folded a bit like paper, and I anticipated a very chewy experience. I was glad to find it was just about as soft as the rest of the pie itself.

It's odd, though. Tasty but odd. South End Grill's pie is far more similar in flavor to an old-fashioned Chick-O-Stick than, say, a peanut butter cup or sandwich. I haven't encountered one similar anywhere else.

If you'd like to try it out (and maybe have one of those oversized dinners), make your way to Highway 167 south of Batesville; it's on the east side of the road south of the airport.

Toasted Coconut Pie at the Feed Lot

Caraway has quite a history. This little burg out east of Jonesboro today is a pretty little place in the road, but back in its heyday, it was where it was happening in that little section of the Delta. Originally known as White Switch, the community used to be the termination point of a railroad spur, and even today, it's known for its cotton farming. The town's big claim to fame: the All-American Red Heads, a professional women's basketball team best known for playing by men's basketball rules and winning 70 percent of its games.

Toasted coconut pie at the Feed Lot in Caraway. *Kat Robinson.*

Elise Staggs is no redhead, but she is a fiery wonder for the town. As manager of the Feed Lot, she sees the bulk of folks who eat around those parts (that would make all of them) and serves them up good vittles. It's always fish on Friday, there's always a mess of fresh Arkansas vegetables on the menu and the fried chicken makes the list for some of the best in the state.

Elise also knows how to get good people to come work for her—as evidenced by resident pie maker Kim Couch. Her specialty is a toasted coconut pie, which blends the best of a coconut cream pie and an icebox pie. Kim starts with a layer of toasted coconut on the bottom of her pressed graham cracker crust. She blends together cream cheese, Eagle brand condensed milk and Cool Whip with a little more toasted coconut and then tops the mess with salted pecans, caramel sauce and even more toasted coconut. It's smooth and rich and the perfect ending to a country lunch.

Possum pie at PattiCakes in Conway. *Grav Weldon*.

PART VII

The Case for Possum Pie

Should it be named the official Arkansas state pie?

Playin' Possum

A quest for the perfect Arkansas dessert turns up all sorts of similar yet happy returns.

I traveled to every corner in the state for this book. I went to Blytheville and Texarkana, Gravette and Lake Village, and I searched for pie everywhere. And everywhere I went, I found this one oddly named proprietary pie.

Now, I will say, you can find coconut meringue pie all over the state. You can find pecan and chocolate cream and sweet potato—all of which have been claimed here and there. But the one that crosses every line, shows up on menus just about everywhere is an Arkansas delicacy known as possum pie.

No, it does not contain real possums, though I once posted a piece to "Eat Arkansas" containing a recipe involving possum's milk that drew a fair bit of attention. It accompanied a "Tie Dye Travels" piece on possum farming in the Delta, which drew the attention of the USDA…did I mention I put these pieces up on April Fool's Day?

Neveryoumind.

The real possum pie is so named because the pie "plays possum"—in this case, representing itself as something else. The traditional pie starts with a sandy bottom, a mix of flour and pecan pieces pressed directly into the pie pan and blind baked before assembly. The rest of the pie isn't baked (usually, though I have seen a few versions that did bake the custard before the rest went on). Into the crust goes a soured cream cheese layer, and then on top of that goes a layer of rich chocolate custard. On top, a layer of whipped cream hides the chocolate layer. It's traditionally topped with pecan bits. If

PattiCakes in Conway. *Grav Weldon*.

you don't know the chocolate is in there, it looks like some sort of strange pecan cream pie hybrid.

It also goes by other names. In southwest Arkansas, I have found it several times listed as a chocolate torte, though there's nothing torte-ish about the pie at all. My friend Kim Williams, when I described it to her, told me in the Delta it's usually called a four-layer delight. Over there, as in other places around and abouts, it's made in a square or rectangular casserole dish rather than a pie pan. But for the most part, the ingredients remain the same.

The initial possum pie I encountered years ago (that is, outside of the chocolate torte version I had many times as a child) was at Stoby's of Russellville. There are two Stoby's restaurants; they're run by David and Patti Stobaugh, and they've received a lot of attention, thanks to an eponymous cheese dip and a musician by the name of Kris Allen, a Conway boy who happened to win a little contest on FOX known as *American Idol*. Kris loved the cheese dip, and when he won, the Stobaughs rewarded him with a lifetime supply. I am assuming it's more of a thing where they'll give him cheese dip whenever he wants; I can't imagine what you'd have to do to store that much cheese dip, considering how much my usual crowd consumes when it's available. Oh bother, I have really rolled way out on a tangent.

Anyway, I went to college at Arkansas Tech University up in Russellville, and whenever there were special occasions, Stoby's was the place to go. It's located in an old building beside the railroad tracks and includes a couple of dining cars along the side. If you're a kid (and maybe if you're not, since I've done it), you can request to blow the train whistle. There are model trains that circle overhead on tracks, and there are burgers and plate dinners and breakfasts. I love the Northerner for breakfast, with its corned beef hash and…

I went off on another tangent there.

Anyway, the possum pie at Stoby's is a standout. Unlike most others, it comes on a flour crust but with pecans incorporated into the cream cheese layer. No matter. It's cool and creamy and usually sells out by the end of the day.

So, Stoby's. The original restaurant was started back in 1980 in Conway. Not long after, the Russellville location was started up, and both thrived. They each obtained a very different vibe, which is to be expected. Both are in college towns, and each has been adopted by the university nearby. Desserts, like everything else, were made in the kitchen.

That is until October 2006, when Patti decided to start up a bakery. PattiCakes began next to the Stoby's in Russellville in yet another old building by the tracks. The place specialized at first in custom cakes and marvelous fudge. But it also started turning out baked goods for Stoby's, including rolls, buns and pies.

In 2010, Patti started a second PattiCakes in Conway, right behind Stoby's there. This new location offered a lot more—doughnuts, cookies and a selection of cold items like chicken salad and tuna salad to take home. And Patti expanded her selection to include even more pies, like the pecan and chocolate Kentucky Derby pie, an amazingly light and rich peanut butter pie and, of course, the possum pie.

Mind you, there are other places you have to mention when you're talking about possum pie. You can't stop with Stoby's and PattiCakes. You have to move on to the different regions of the state, spread out and cover the area and share all those great possum pie locations.

You actually start right across the tracks there in Russellville at a little place called Opal Mae's. It's a little hole in the wall I've just fallen in love with. The place got started when Dennis Martin left Cagle's Mill, a longtime Russellville fine dining experience. Dennis had one specialty: he made the best prime rib in the state. He still does, in my opinion.

Martin named his little restaurant on B Street after his mom and got started. It's open for lunch during the week, selling family-style dinners served either at the little buffet or brought to your table for you to share with the folks you came with. At night, it's a finer dining experience, made doubly so by the fact that the little place only has about seven tables.

Now, there are some full-sized desserts served at Martin's place, but not a lot. He likes to make little desserts—little divine lemon cakes (which I adore), tiny chocolate bombs, cookies and, of course, the tiny flowerpot pies. These are pie shots—at least, that's what everyone calls them these days. Martin was doing these for at least five years before the pie shot idea really took off around here. Among those shots, you'll find a possum pie. His starts with a pecan sandy cookie instead of a bottom crust. Then it's the same soured cream cheese layer, the same chocolate layer, still topped with whipped cream and pecan pieces. Best of all, it's about half what you'd get in a traditional pie slice, so you can have two. The pie can be found elsewhere in town, too, at the venerable Old South on Main Street and who-all knows where else.

Head on west out I-40 toward Lamar, a little spot on the road north of the interstate. Take U.S. 64 into town and right inside a curve, right by the post office, you'll find a little lunchroom called Sweet Treats. Rex Nelson turned me on to this place and claimed it has the best pie in the state. Well, the pies there are pretty good.

Every day Monday through Friday, Sweet Treats serves up a single lunch special with a choice of sides. The place also does cold sandwiches and chili and a chef's salad, and always there are a number of pies on the board. My favorite? Strangely enough, not the possum pie but the caramel pecan pie. It's a pecan pie made with sugar instead of Karo syrup. It comes across as the bastard child of a pecan pie and a burnt sugar pie without the meringue, and it's dadgum good, very praline-ish and crisp.

Sweet Treats' possum pie goes a layer further to hide its chocolate: it has a cream cheese layer both above and below the chocolate custard, which ups the decadence level severely. It's also on a flour crust like Stoby's but without the pecans in the cream cheese layer.

You could eat your way up I-40 on possum pie at so many of the restaurants I've already talked about: Hillbilly Hideout in Ozark, Red Rooster Bistro in Alma and even down into Fort Smith, Greenwood and south along U.S. 71. Take on the Northwest Corridor, though, and you have even more pies to savor. A number of good possum pies lie within a breath of U.S. 71 B between Fayetteville and Bella Vista, all worthy in their own way. In northwest Arkansas, possum pie tends to be a square affair.

The largest possum pie slice I have encountered by far is offered at Sassy's Red House in Fayetteville. The popular stop for Arkansas Razorback fans is known for its barbecue sauce, dry smoked ribs and burgers, and the pie is huge. It almost misses the pie definition, being a quarter of a quarter sheet

Possum pie at Sweet Treats in Lamar. *Kat Robinson*.

pan's worth of acreage. But there is a crust, a thick pecan sandy crust topped with a very rich and thick layer of sweetened cream cheese, a layer of light chocolate pudding, another cream cheese layer, a layer of whipped cream and a good sprinkle of crumbled pecans. Sweet, irresistible and light—and extraordinarily huge. A sharing pie five to six inches square.

Up the road in Springdale and over a bit on U.S. 412, you'll find the Front Porch Diner. There are always pies on the menu there that vary day by day—meringues and creams and chiffons, oh my. There, it's not just a possum pie, it's the Awesome Possum pie, and there is good reason for the name. A casserole-type pie, this possum pie starts with a very thick sandy crust, onto which is smeared the lightest cream cheese layer. Piled on this is a thick layer of dark, almost bittersweet chocolate custard, so rich it colors the layer below it a delicate pink. Topped with whipped cream only when served, it packs a lot of flavor in a small package.

Of course, you have other possum pie locations, especially the incredible Myrtie Mae's up in Eureka Springs. At the Rambler Café in Rose Bud, they make theirs like almost everyone else, but it's called the opossum pie (of course, the "o" is silent).

And you can find it in central Arkansas, notably at places like Hunka Pie in North Little Rock and at Paula Lynn's Really Homemade Sandwich & Sweet Shop in Bryant, though at the latter it's called the Chocolate Dream and omits the whipped cream on top. In fact, the Chocolate Dream is actually a fantastic chocolate mousse on top of a cloud of delightfully light cream cheese in a double-layered blind-baked flour crust. Without the whipped cream on top, you can tell what it is, so you can't really call it a possum pie, but it tastes so very, very similar.

You'll find possum pie in other places, too, in Arkansas' deep south, in finer restaurants and in grungy hole-in-the-wall sort of places. Barr's Junction isn't grungy, but it is the only game in town in the tiny southwest Arkansas burg of Rosston. It's at the Y in the road, and if you get to Rosston, you will see the low-slung white building in that Y's crook. It's everything to the community—grocery, sporting goods store, convenience store and restaurant.

It was toward the end of the research for the *Arkansas Times* cover story, toward the end of a long weekend spent covering a festival and looking for burgers and pies in south Arkansas. We were on our way back from El Dorado and needed beverages for the return trip to Little Rock—and I needed to make a pit stop.

After taking care of my business, I went to get my beverage and was advised I needed to check with the woman behind the counter. That nice lady told me she'd already sold out two of her pies that day, but she had one more in the back and would I like a slice? Well, of course I would.

What I received was not an angled slice but a square that had been cut from the dessert in its nine- by thirteen-inch Pyrex baking pan. She called it a chocolate torte, but I instantly recognized it for what it was: a beautifully formed and crafted possum pie. Everything was there—the sandy flour-pecan bottom, the cream cheese custard, the pudding-like chocolate and whipped cream on top. And it was good, too.

So that's a lot of possum pie. Question is, is it the official Arkansas pie? Well, not yet. Truthfully, there is no such thing as the official state pie of Arkansas; it's never been determined (much to the chagrin of the Cliff House Inn). Should it be?

I was doing research on my big pie cover story for the *Arkansas Times* in the fall of 2011, and I did my queries and searches. As far as anyone at the state capital, the Arkansas History Commission or the Historic Arkansas Museum knows, there really isn't a state pie. And it was suggested to me that I start a campaign to make the possum pie the official state pie of Arkansas.

But I have so many irons in the fire. And I think naming one pie to that honor is going to tick someone off. After all, determining a single instance of pie above all others and calling it the official pie is like to cause political trouble. And I'm not one to start a fight.

Chocolate torte at Barr's Junction in Rosston. *Grav Weldon.*

Of course, what you've been really been waiting for all this time is a recipe. Here's mine:

Possum Pie

1½ sticks butter

2 cups flour

2 cups crushed pecans, separated

1 8-ounce package cream cheese, room temperature

1 cup confectioners' sugar

12 ounces Cool Whip, divided

1 box milk chocolate instant pudding

1 box chocolate fudge instant pudding

3 cups milk

Heat oven to 350°. Cut butter into flour to make crumbly pastry dough. Add 1 cup crushed pecans. Press into two 8- or 9-inch pie pans or one 13- by 9-inch casserole. Bake 15 minutes or until flour starts to brown. Remove and cool.

Cream together cream cheese and confectioners' sugar. Add six ounces of Cool Whip and beat until fluffy. Spread over bottom of both pies.

Blend together both pudding mixes with milk. Pour in on top of the cream cheese mixture and allow to set.

Spread remaining Cool Whip over the top of both pies and sprinkle with pecans. Makes two pies.

Myrtie Mae's

Ninety years of fried chicken and who knows how many of pie—Myrtie Mae's serves up both and still does it swell.

Good fried chicken can be found in select locations in Arkansas. One of those places has been making fried chicken the same way for ninety years on a highway corner in Eureka Springs—and thank goodness they serve pie too.

The place: Myrtie Mae's, a town institution. The restaurant's namesake was a spry woman who made the best of needing to raise six kids on her own. She did it with Ozark fried chicken.

Tourism really started to take hold in the Arkansas Ozarks back in the 1920s with the spread of the automobile. Eureka Springs drew people to the Ozarks with its springs and its resemblance to the Swiss Alps, perched on hillsides above valleys and vistas. Travelers would make their way to the town through some crazy terrain and then set up camp. One of those campgrounds was located at what is now the corner of U.S. 62 and Midway (the old U.S. 62 Business loop) on the northwest side of town. Campers paid a quarter a night for the privilege to pitch their tents.

Well, folks have to eat, and though most travelers were somewhat self-sufficient and had their own beans-in-a-can or similar meal to take care of themselves, the idea of a hot meal someone else cooked was tempting. Enter Myrtie Mae. The widow and mother of six nailed a sign advertising "Home-Style Chicken Dinners" to a tree in front of her place (close to

Possum pie at Myrtie Mae's in Eureka Springs. *Kat Robinson.*

where the restaurant is today) and served people at her own dining room table. She whipped up mashed potatoes, cream gravy, jams and jellies and vegetables and, of course, her own recipe of fried chicken. Myrtie could purportedly see who was coming to dinner, go out and kill and dress a young chicken, prepare it and have it on the table in thirty minutes' time. Talk about fresh.

But what does all this have to do with pie? Well, it has to do with the restaurant today. Myrtie's no longer with us—I mean, it has been ninety-some-odd years since those first dinners were sold!—but the tradition continues at the Best Western Inn of the Ozarks at the restaurant that bears her name.

I went in one evening and ordered up Myrtie's Famous Ozark Fried Chicken. My kind waitress directed me to the soup and salad bar to partake before the main course. In addition to the traditional salad bar, there are two soups offered each day (this time it was vegetable and a cream of asparagus with ham), lots of congealed sort of mixed salads like ambrosia and Jell-O fruit

Myrtie Mae's fried chicken. *Kat Robinson.*

salad and fresh-baked breads. I selected a cute heart-shaped blueberry muffin and a small jalapeño corn bread sphere to whet my appetite.

The waitress brought out this nice soft loaf of dark brown bread. It was just slightly sweet but definitely in need of butter, which was provided in a huge bowl of individually wrapped pats on the table.

Out came the chicken, which I smelled before it reached the table. The three oversized pieces just about crowded out the side of broccoli on my plate (they do have other options, like baked potatoes, whipped potatoes, French fries and rice pilaf; I was just being good). There was silverware on the table, but I'm a southern gal. I just picked up that chicken leg in front of me and went to town.

And it's very good chicken, the fourth best I've had in the state (after Dew-Baby's in Stuttgart, AQ Chicken House in Springdale and the Monte Ne Inn Chicken Restaurant). It wasn't so juicy that I had to sop up grease, but it was juicy enough to need to dab the corners of my mouth. I ended up saving the chicken thigh that came with the meal for later. Oh, and if you do order, you get three pieces of their choice. You want all light or all dark? It's a buck more.

So we come to the pie. There are always pies on the dessert list at Myrtie Mae's, chocolate and coconut cream pies and a fruit pie of whatever's in season. And then there's the possum pie, which fits the possum pie directive. Yes, it contained the prerequisite cream cheese and chocolate layers, the sandy bottomed crust and the whipped cream top—and it also had a nice drizzle of chocolate sauce to go along with the sprinkled pecans on the top.

Thing is, the food is pretty good, especially considering the prices. There are more expensive items on the menu, such as the steaks and the fish at dinnertime, but really, if you're going to go, try that fried chicken that's still made with Myrtie Mae's recipe. Pretty darn good.

You'll find Myrtie Mae's in Eureka Springs at the Best Western Inn of the Ozarks Conference Center. It's on the east side of town on U.S. 62. Just look for the water wheel out front.

Appendix I

A Few More Recipes

Ashley Lavender's Caramel Bottom Peach Pie

2 tablespoons butter
2 tablespoons flour
¾ cup evaporated milk
I cup sugar
½ teaspoon salt
I pie crust (I buy the frozen deep-dish kind)
2 cups fresh peaches (about 6–7 medium peaches)
16 ounces whipped topping (Cool Whip)

Make a paste over the stove with the butter and flour. Add in evaporated milk, then the sugar and salt. Heat until thickened.
Pour into baked pie crust and then put in the fridge for an hour or so to cool.
Skin and slice peaches and combine with Cool Whip (reserving one cup's worth).
When pie crust and caramel mix is solid, add peaches. Frost with remaining Cool Whip. Refrigerate until ready to serve.

Ms. Lena's Squash Pie
Courtesy of Viv Barnhill

2 eggs
2 cups milk
¾ cup sugar
I cup cooked squash
½ teaspoon salt
½ teaspoon pumpkin pie spice
½ teaspoon vanilla

Blend all ingredients. Pour into pre-baked pie shell and bake at 375° for 30 minutes or until knife comes out clean.

Bradley County Pink Tomato Pie
Submitted by Angela Norton

I 9-inch deep-dish pie shell
3–5 large tomatoes, peeled, sliced to about ½ inch thick
  (remove the seeds)
½ teaspoon salt
½ teaspoon pepper
additional herbs if wanted: basil, parsley, garlic salt, etc.
I cup mayonnaise
¾ cup grated cheddar cheese
¾ cup grated mozzarella cheese
¼ cup scallions or chives
6 strips cooked bacon (optional)

Bake pie shell for 10 minutes at 375°. Layer tomatoes in shell and sprinkle with salt, pepper and additional herbs and spices if wanted.
Mix together mayonnaise, cheese and scallions/chives. Spread mixture over tomatoes in pie shell. Bake at 350° for 30 minutes until brown and bubbly. Crumble bacon on top. Allow to stand 5 minutes before serving.

Zack Diemer's Cherry Cream Cheese Pie

My brother has the task each holiday season of creating a pie, and this is the usual suspect: the traditional cherry-pie-filling-topped favorite done large. He makes it up in a Tupperware Large White Round Storage Container (Tupperseal) that outdates both of us. The thing is thirteen inches in diameter and about three inches tall. You can substitute four eight-inch pie pans instead.

1 box graham crackers, pounded to crumbs
4 8-ounce packages cream cheese, room temperature
2 14-ounce cans sweetened condensed milk
1 tablespoon vanilla extract
1 cup lemon juice
2 21-ounce cans cherry pie filling

If you haven't done it already, beat the hell out of the graham crackers until they're big moist crumbs of graham cracker dirt. Press into the bottom of the Tupperware container. Set aside.

Beat the tar out of the cream cheese until it's sorta fluffy. Add in everything else but the cherries. Make sure the lumps are out. Slide into the fridge and let chill for four hours. Top with the cherry pie filling and serve. If you feel really fancy, get a can of cherry pie filling and a can of blueberry pie filling and go nuts with it.

The Incomplete Compendium of Great Arkansas Pie Places

302 ON THE SQUARE
302 Public Square
Berryville, AR 72616
(870) 654-3952
www.ozarts.org
Dang Good Pie
Northwest

65TH STREET DINER
3201 West 65th Street
Little Rock, AR 72209
(501) 562-7800
Coconut meringue
Central

ADAM'S CATFISH WAGON
215 North Cross Street
Perryville, AR 72201
(501) 374-4265
www.PleaseEatFish.com
Fried pies
Central

ALLEY OOPS
11900 Kanis Road #D10
Little Rock, AR 72211
(501) 224-9400
Chess pie and chocolate chess pie
Central

AMISH AND COUNTRY STORE
3040 U.S. 65 North
Dermott, AR 71638
(870) 538-9990
Fried pies
Delta/southeast

ASHLEY'S AT THE CAPITAL
111 West Markham
Little Rock, AR 72201
(501) 374-7474
www.capitalhotel.com/Ashleyswebsite
Buttermilk tart, fried pies and more
Central

ATKINSON'S BLUE DIAMOND CAFÉ
1800 East Harding
Morrilton, AR 72110
(501) 354-4253
Chocolate meringue
Central

BABYCAKES
4117 U.S. 62
Mountain Home, AR 72653
(870) 405-6939
www.Facebook.com/BabycakesFriedPies
Fried pies
North central

THE BACKYARD BBQ COMPANY
1407 East Main Street
Magnolia, AR 71753
(870) 234-7890
Various pies
South central

BALCONY RESTAURANT AT THE BASIN PARK HOTEL
12 Spring Street
Eureka Springs, AR 72632
(479) 253-7837
www.basinpark.com
Huckleberry pie
Northwest

BARKER'S FAMILY RESTAURANT
112 South Edmonds Avenue
McCrory, AR 72101
(870) 731-2999
Chocolate and coconut meringue pies
Delta/northeast

BARR'S JUNCTION
6683 Highway 278
Rosston, AR 72858
(870) 871-2426
Chocolate torte (variant of possum pie)
Southwest

BATTEN'S BAKERY
230 East Kingshighway
Paragould, AR 72450
(870) 236-7810
Old Fashioned Chocolate Pie
Delta/northeast

BENNY BOB'S BBQ
841 East Main Street
Blytheville, AR 72315
(870) 763-0505
Fried pies
Delta/northeast

BETTY'S STEAK & CHICKEN
1203 North Illinois
Harrisburg, AR 72432
(870) 578-2855
Apple pie
Delta/northeast

BIG JAKE'S BBQ
1521 Arkansas Boulevard
Texarkana, AR 71854
(870) 774-0099
www.BigJakesBBQ.com
Fried pies
Southwest

BIG JOHN'S SHAKE SHACK
409 Military Road
Marion, AR 72364
(870) 739-3943
Traditional and fried pies
Delta/east

BIG SPRINGS TRADING COMPANY
14237 North U.S. 65
St. Joe, AR 72675
(870) 439-2900
www.bigspringstradingco.com
Traditional pies
Northwest

BOARDWALK CAFÉ
401B West Court Street
Jasper, AR 72641
(479) 446-5900
www.thearkhouse.com
Ozark black walnut pie
Northwest

BOB AND WANDA'S JENNY LIND COUNTRY CAFÉ
2655 Gate Nine Road
Greenwood, AR 72936
(501) 996-1099
Various pies
West

BOBBY'S COUNTRY COOKING
301 North Shackleford Road #E1
Little Rock, AR 72211
(501) 224-9500
www.bobbyscountrycookin.com
Various traditional pies
Central

BOURBON STREET STEAKHOUSE
Inside Southland Gaming and Racing
1550 Ingram Boulevard
West Memphis, AR 72301
(870) 735-3670
www.SouthlandPark.com
Bourbon pecan pie, Key lime pie
Delta/east

THE BRICKHOUSE DINER
1606 Page
Malvern, AR 72104
(501) 337-5050
Various pies
Southwest

BROWN BAG KITCHEN
119 Stephenson
Harrison, AR 72601
(870) 688-8552
https://www.facebook.com/pages/The-Brown-Bag-
Kitchen/291476914224116?v=info
Various pies
Northwest

BROWN SUGAR BAKESHOP
419 East Third Street
Little Rock, AR 72201
(501) 372-4009
www.brownsugarbakeshop.com
Oreo pie
Central

BULLDOG RESTAURANT
3614 Highway 367 North
Bald Knob, AR 72010
(501) 724-5195
Coconut meringue
Delta/northeast

BURGERS-N-MORE
148 Amity Road
Hot Springs, AR 71913
(501) 525-0919
Southwest

BURGE'S HICKORY SMOKED TURKEYS AND HAMS
Arkansas 29 North
Lewisville, AR 71854
(870) 921-4292
www.SmokedTurkeys.com
Fried pies
Southwest

Burge's in the Heights
5620 R Street
Little Rock, AR 72207
(501) 666-1660
www.SmokedTurkeys.com
Fried pies
Central

Cafe Bossa Nova
2701 Kavanaugh Boulevard
Little Rock, AR 72205
(501) 614-6682
www.cafebossanova.com
Four-layer pie (possum pie)
Central

Cafe 1217
1217 Malvern Avenue #B
Hot Springs, AR 71901
(501) 318-1094
www.cafe1217.net
Various designer pies

Capital Bar and Grill
11 West Markham
Little Rock, AR 72201
(501) 374-7474
www.capitalhotel.com/CBG
Fried pies
Central

Carol's Lakeview Dinette
200 Iroquoi Drive
Cherokee Village, AR 72529
(870) 257-3959
Sugar-free pies

CATALPA CAFÉ
Highway 215
Ozone, AR 72854
(479) 292-3292
CatalpaCafe.blogspot.com
Various pies
Northwest

CATFISH HOLE
4127 West Wedington Drive
Fayetteville, AR 72704
(479) 521-7008
www.TheCatfishHole.com
Fried pies
Northwest

CHARLOTTE'S EATS AND SWEETS
290 Main Street
Keo, AR 72083
(501) 841-2123
Meringue pies
Central

CHEF'S IN
105 Burke Avenue
Jonesboro, AR 72401
(870) 934-8962
Raisin pie
Delta/northeast

CHIP'S BARBECUE
9801 West Markham
Little Rock, AR 72205
(501) 225-4346
Various cream and nut pies
Central

CHUCK'S DINER AND STEAKHOUSE
35 Swinging Bridge Drive

Heber Springs, AR 72543
(501) 362-2100
North central

CHUCK WAGON RESTAURANT
9174 U.S. 65 S.
Bee Branch, AR 72013
(501) 745-8600
Various pies
Northwest

CIAO ITALIAN RESTAURANT
405 West Seventh
Little Rock, AR 72201
(501) 372-0238
www.ciaoitalianrestaurant.com
Key lime pie
Central

CLARA'S MIDWAY CAFÉ
153 Main Street
Tyronza, AR 72386
(870) 487-2090
Delta/northeast

CLIFF HOUSE INN
HC 31 Box 85 (on Highway 7)
Jasper, AR 72641
(870) 446-2292
www.cliffhouseinnar.com
Company's Comin' pie
Northwest

CLUB 178
2109 Central Boulevard
Bull Shoals, AR 72619
(870) 445-4949
www.178club.com
Grasshopper pie
North central

Key lime pie at Community Bakery in Little Rock. *Grav Weldon*.

COLONIAL STEAKHOUSE
111 West Eighth Street
Pine Bluff, AR 71601
(870) 536-3488
Black bottom pie
Delta/southeast

COMMUNITY BAKERY
1200 Main Street
Little Rock, AR 72202
(501) 375-6418
www.communitybakery.com
Central

COTHAM'S IN THE CITY
1401 West Third Street
Little Rock, AR 72201
(501) 370-9177

www.cothamsinthecity.com
Fried pies
Central

COTHAM'S MERCANTILE
5301 Arkansas 161
Scott, AR 72142
(501) 961-9284
www.cothams.com
Fried pies
Central

COUNTRY ROOSTER
101 Phillips Avenue
Green Forest, AR 72638
(870) 438-5710
Meringue pies
Northwest

COUNTRY VILLAGE BAKERY
158 Knight Haven Circle
Star City, AR 71667
(870) 628-3333
Various traditional and fried pies
South central

CRAIG FAMILY BAKERY
805 Fayetteville Road
Van Buren, AR 72956
(479) 471-8800
Fried pies
West

CROSS CREEK SANDWICH SHOP
1003 Oak Street
Conway, AR 72032
(501) 764-1811
Strawberry pie
Central

Dairy King
105 Main Street
Portia, AR 72457
(870) 886-6301
Fried pies
North central

Dan's I-30 Diner
17018 Interstate 30
Benton, AR 72019
(501) 778-4116
Traditional pies
Central

Dave's Place
210 Center Street
Little Rock, AR 72201
(501) 372-3283
www.davesplacerestaurant.com
Central

Delicious Temptations
11200 North Rodney Parham
Little Rock, AR 72212
(501) 225-6893
www.delicioustemptations.com
Bourbon chocolate pecan pie
Central

DeVito's
350 DeVitos Loop
Harrison, AR 72601
(870) 741-8832
www.devitosrestaurant.com
Apple pie and bourbon pecan pie
Northwest

DEW-BABY'S
813 East Michigan
Stuttgart, AR 72160
(870) 672-7333
Egg custard
Delta/southeast

DIANE'S GOURMET LUXURIES
11121 North Rodney Parham
Little Rock, AR 72212
(501) 224-2639
www.dianes-gourmet.com
Dutch apple
Central

DILLARD SHELL
1934 Arkansas 53
Gurdon, AR 71743
(870) 353-2544
Fried pies
Southwest

The Diner in Cabot. *Grav Weldon*.

Coconut cream pie at Dogtown Coffee and Cookery in North Little Rock. *Kat Robinson*.

THE DINER
3286 South Second Street
Cabot, AR 72023
(501) 941-0904
Meringue pies
Central

DOGTOWN COFFEE & COOKERY
6725 John F. Kennedy Boulevard
North Little Rock, AR 72116
(501) 833-3850
www.DogtownCookery.com
Coconut cream pie
Central

DRY CREEK MERCANTILE
21595 U.S. 65
Pindall, AR 72669
(870) 439-8190
www.drycreekhomestead.com
Fresh strawberry pie
Northwest

ED AND KAY'S RESTAURANT
15228 Interstate 30
Benton, AR 72019
(501) 315-3663
Mile-High meringue pies and PCP pie
Central

ED'S CUSTOM BAKERY
256 Oak Street
Conway, AR 72032
(501) 327-2996
Sugar cookie cherry pie
Central

Sugar cookie cherry pie at Ed's Custom Bakery in Conway. *Kat Robinson*.

EMERSON'S GROCERY
PO Box 182
Rover, AR 72860
(479) 272-4177
Fried pies
West

E'S BISTRO
3812 John F. Kennedy Boulevard
North Little Rock, AR 72116
(501) 771-6900
www.esbistronlr.com
Lemon pecan pie and Hershey pie
Central

FAMILY PIE SHOP
Highway 70 West
DeValls Bluff, AR 72041
(870) 998-2279
Traditional and fried pies
Delta/east

FAT DAWGZ BBQ AND SOMETHING SWEET
108 Fulton
Clarksville, AR 72830
(479) 754-2857
www.facebook.com/pages/Fat-Dawgz-BBQ-Something-Sweet/182771221737100
Frozen peanut butter pie
West

FAYRAYS
100 East Elm Street
El Dorado, AR 71730
(870) 863-4000
www.fayrayseldorado.com
Bourbon pecan pie
South central

THE FEED LOT
103 East State Street
Caraway, AR 72419
(870) 956-0055
Toasted coconut pie
Delta/northeast

FISHERMAN'S WHARF
5101 Central Avenue
Hot Springs, AR 71913
(501) 525-7437
www.fishermanswharfhs.com
Key lime pie
Southwest

FLY WHEEL'S PIES
1655 Highway 19 North
Prescott, AR 71857
(870) 887-5367
Fried pies by order only
Southwest

FOX CREEK BBQ
129 Lawrence Street
Batesville, AR 72501
(870) 698-0034
www.FoxCreekBBQ.com
Fried pies
North central

FRANKE'S CAFETERIA
11121 North Rodney Parham
Little Rock, AR 72212
(501) 225-4487
www.frankescafeteria.com
Cinnamon cream pie
Central

FRED'S COUNTRY COOKIN'
16538 U.S. 71
Boles, AR 72926
(479) 577-2676
Fried pies
West

FRONT PORCH FAMILY DINER
669 East Robinson Avenue
Springdale, AR 72764
(479) 751-3021
https://www.facebook.com/FrontPorchDiner
Awesome Possum pie
Northwest

GIBB'S GROCERY
7781 Highway 167 South
Sheridan, AR 72150
(870) 942-5284
Various pies
South central

GINA'S PLACE
2005 East Highland, Suite 109
Jonesboro, AR 72401
(870) 910-3900
www.eatatanns.com
Peanut butter pie
Delta/northeast

GODSEY'S GRILL
226 South Main Street
Jonesboro, AR 72401
(870) 336-1988
www.godseysgrill.com
Peanut butter icebox
Delta/northeast

GRANDMA'S HOUSE CAFÉ
21588 U.S. 71
Winslow, AR 72959
(479) 634-2128
Various pies
Northwest

GRANDPA'S BBQ
2008 North Second Street
Cabot, AR 72023
(501) 941-1141
www.grandpasbarbeque.com
Pecan fried pie
Central

GREENHOUSE GRILLE
481 South School
Fayetteville, AR 72701
(479) 474-8909
www.greenhousegrille.com
Bourbon chocolate chunk pecan
Northwest

HAROLD'S BAR-B-Q AND LOUNGE
4897 Malvern Road
Hot Springs, AR 71901
(501) 262-3032
Southwest

HILLBILLY HIDEOUT
I-40 Travel Center
Exit 35, I-40
Ozark, AR 72949
(479) 667-0711
Various pies
West

HOLLY'S COUNTRY COOKING
120 Harkrider
Conway, AR 72032
(501) 328-9738
Banana cream pie
Central

THE HOUSE
722 North Palm
Little Rock, AR 72205
(501) 663-4500
www.thehouseinhillcrest.com
"The Best Key Lime Pie"
Central

HUNKA PIE
250 Military Drive
North Little Rock, AR 72118
(501) 612-4754
www.hunkapie.com
Various pies
Central

HURLEY HOUSE CAFÉ
1303 Highway 70 West
Hazen, AR 72064
(870) 255-4679
Fried pies
Delta/east

J&S ITALIAN VILLA
4332 Central Avenue, Suite B
Hot Springs, AR 71913
(501) 525-1121
www.jandsitalianvilla.com
Key lime pie
Southwest

JAVA PRIMO
4429 Central Avenue
Hot Springs, AR 71913
(501) 318-9789
www.javaprimo.com
Sweet potato almond streusel
Southwest

JUST LIKE MOM'S
3140 East Kiehl Avenue
Sherwood, AR 72120
(501) 833-0402
www.justlikemoms.us
Various pies
Central

KATHERINE'S CAFE AMORE
2070 East Van Buren
Eureka Springs, AR 72632
(479) 253-7192
www.cafeamorearkansas.com
Cream cheese pies
Northwest

KIRBY RESTAURANT
2860 U.S. 70 West
Kirby, AR 71950
(870) 398-4441
West

LETHA'S FRIED PIES
88 North Centennial, Suite 3
West Fork, AR 72774
(479) 387-5011
Northwest

LEWIS FAMILY RESTAURANT
5901 Highway 71 South
Fort Smith, AR 72908
(479) 646-4309
Various pies
West

LINDSEY'S HOSPITALITY HOUSE
207 Curtis Sykes Drive
North Little Rock, AR 72114
(501) 374-5707
www.lindseysbbqnmore.com
Sweet potato, egg custard and fried pies
Central

LITTLE HANNAH'S BAKE SHOPPE
6729 Heber Springs Road North
Drasco, AR 72530
(870) 668-9190
North central

Lucy's Diner
4605 Towson Avenue
Fort Smith, AR 72901
(479) 646-1000
Various pies
West

Luigi's Pizza and Pasta
22200 Interstate 30
Bryant, AR 72022
(501) 847-1110
www.LuigisBryant.org
Blueberry pie
Central

Lunchbox
1100 East Race Avenue
Searcy, AR
(501) 268-4040
Traditional and fried pies
North central

Mack's Fish House
559 Wilburn Road
Heber Springs, AR 72543
(501) 362-6225
www.MacksFishHouse.com
North central

Mama Max's
1102 West Main
Prescott, AR 71857
(870) 887-5005
Various pies
Southwest

MAMA Z'S
357 West Henri de Tonti Boulevard
Tontitown, AR 72762
(479) 361-2750
Chocolate and coconut meringue pie
Northwest

MARTHA JEAN'S DINER
5419 Arkansas 367
Beebe, AR 72012
(501) 882-3100
Peanut butter chocolate meringue
Central

MARY MAESTRI'S
669 East Robinson
Springdale, AR 72762
(479) 756-1441
www.marymaestris.com
Chocolate cream pie
Northwest

MATHER LODGE AT PETIT JEAN STATE PARK
1069 Petit Jean Mountain Road
Morrilton, AR 72110
(501) 727-5604
www.PetitJeanStatePark.com
Lemon icebox pie
West

MAXINE'S SOUTHERN FRIED PIES
2136 Airport Road
Hot Springs, AR 71913
(501) 760-2565
Fried pies
Southwest

MIKE'S PLACE
808 Front Street
Conway, AR 72032
(501) 269-6453
www.MikesPlaceConway.com
Central

MISS ANNA'S ON TOWSON
5001 Towson Avenue
Fort Smith, AR 72901
(479) 649-6300
Various pies
West

MISTY'S SHELL
U.S. 65 North
Leslie, AR 72645
(870) 447-2544
Fried pies
Northwest

MOUNT IDA CAFE
978 U.S. 270
Mount Ida, AR 71957
Blueberry and Rocky Road pies
Southwest

MS. LENA'S
Highway 33 North
DeValls Bluff, AR 72041
(870) 998-1393
Whole and fried pies
Delta/east

Mud Street Café
22 South Main Street #G
Eureka Springs, AR 72632
(479) 253-6732
www.mudstreetcafe.com
Various cream pies
Northwest

Mustang Sally's
303 West Main Street
Perryville, AR 72176
(501) 889-1501
Fried pies
Central

Myrtie Mae's
207 West Van Buren
Eureka Springs, AR 72632
(479) 253-9768
www.myrtiemaes.com
Possum pie
Northwest

Nana's Diner
1132 North Washington Street
Forrest City, AR 72335
(870) 494-4999
Strawberry pie
Delta/east

Neale's Café
806 North Thompson
Springdale, AR 72764
(479) 751-9996
www.nealscafe.com
Toasted topped meringue pies
Northwest

Nick's BBQ and Catfish
1012 North Bankhead Drive
Highway 13 North
Carlisle, AR 72024
(870) 552-3887
www.nicksbbq.com
Pecan pie and fried pies
Central

Oark General Store
10360 County Road 5440
Ozone, AR 72854
(479) 292-3351
www.oarkgeneralstore.com
Various pies
Northwest

O'Henry's
283 Highway 365
Conway, AR 72032
(501) 470-9045
Buttermilk pie
Central

Old Tyme Burger
1205 Arkansas Boulevard
Texarkana, AR 71854
(870) 772-5775
Southwest

Opal Mae's
321 West B Street
Russellville, AR 72801
(479) 967-6725
www.opalmaescafe.com
Flowerpot pies, possum pie
West

Original Fried Pie Shop
1321 T.P. White Drive
Jacksonville, AR 72076
(501) 985-0508
www.TheOriginalFriedPieShop.com
Fried pies
Central

Overcup Diner
2723 Highway 9 North
Morrilton, AR 72110
(501) 354-9998
Peanut butter pie
Northwest

Papa Joe's
12295 U.S. 165
Humnoke, AR 72072
(501) 275-8000
www.papajoescountrystoreandcafe.com
Coconut meringue pie
Delta/southeast

Parker Pioneer Homestead
16738 Homestead Road
Harrisburg, AR 72432
(870) 578-2699
www.ParkerHomestead.com
Fried pies (October only)
Delta/northeast

Pat's Place
2104 South Main Street
Stuttgart, AR 72160
(870) 672-7770
Chocolate meringue pie
Delta/southeast

PattiCakes
2106 Robinson Avenue
Conway, AR 72034
(501) 205-1969
www.PattiCakesBakery.net
Various pies
Central

Patty's Down the Road
6920 Albert Pike
Hot Springs, AR 71968
(501) 881-4668
www.PattysDownTheRoadHotSprings.com
Southwest

Paula Lynn's Really Homemade Sandwich & Sweet Shop
304 North Reynolds Road
Bryant, AR 72022
(501) 847-2066
www.PaulaLynns.com
Chocolate Dream pie (possum pie variant)
Central

Paul's Bakery
1800 Main Street
Van Buren, AR 72956
(479) 474-7044
West

Pickens Commisary
1000 Pickens Road
Dumas, AR 71639
(870) 382-5266
Fresh strawberry pie, fried pies
Delta/southeast

Piggy Sue's
521 Highway 425 South
Monticello, AR 71655

(870) 367-8466
Fried pies
Delta/south central

Poppy's Diner
301 Greenwood Avenue
Lepanto, AR 72354
(870) 475-3826
Cherry cream cheese fried pie
Delta/northeast

Ralph's Pink Flamingo BBQ
2801 Old Greenwood Road
Fort Smith, AR 72903
(479) 642-7247
www.pinkflamingobbq.com
Chocolate bourbon pecan pie

Rambler Café
442 Highway 5
Rose Bud, AR 72137
(501) 556-4262
Peanut butter pie
North central

Ray's Dairy Maid (Barton)
5322 U.S. 49
West Helena, AR 72390
(870) 572-3060
Nana Deane's Coconut Pecan Pie, fried pies
Delta/southeast

Ray's Drive-In
207 Highway 425 North
Monticello, AR 71655
(870) 367-3292
Fried pies
Delta/south central

RED OAK FILLIN' STATION
2169 Carpenter Dam Road
Hot Springs, AR 71913
(501) 262-0400
Pineapple Delight pie
Southwest

RED ROOSTER BISTRO
221 Highway 71 North
Alma, AR 72921
(479) 430-7518
Various pies
West

RHODA'S FAMOUS HOT TAMALES
714 Saint Mary Street
Lake Village, AR 71653
(870) 265-3108
Mini-pies and fried pies
Delta/southeast

RISON COUNTRY STORE
1980 U.S. 63
Rison, AR 71665
(870) 357-8259
Fried pies
Delta/south central

RITA'S
10894 Highway 27
Hector, AR 72843
(479) 284-3000
Lemon icebox pie
West

ROLANDO'S RESTAURANTE
210 Central Avenue
Hot Springs, AR 71901
(501) 318-6054
www.rolandosrestaurante.com
Key lime pie
Southwest

ROLLING PIN CAFÉ
2565 East Huntsville Road
Fayetteville, AR 72701
(479) 521-3855
www.RollingPinCafe.com
Northwest

RON'S BBQ
326 Highway 70 East
Glenwood, AR 71943
(870) 356-5250
www.facebook.com/RonsBBQ
Coconut and chocolate meringue
Southwest

SAM'S OLD TIME HAMBURGERS
120 East Locust Street
Rogers, AR 72756
(479) 986-9191
Northwest

SASSY'S RED HOUSE
708 North College
Fayetteville, AR 72701
(479) 856-6366
www.sassysredhouse.com
Possum pie
Northwest

THE SHACK
7901 Arkansas 7
Jessieville, AR 71949
(501) 984-5619
Southwest

SHANGRI-LA RESORT
975 Shangri Lane
Mount Ida, AR 71957
(501) 867-2011
www.shangrilaresortar.com
Various fruit and meringue pies
Southwest

SIM'S BAR-B-QUE
1307 Barrow Road
Little Rock, AR 72204
(501) 224-2057
2415 Broadway Street
Little Rock, AR 72206
(501) 732-6868
www.simsbarbeque-ar.com
Sweet potato pie
Central

THE SKILLET RESTAURANT AT THE OZARK FOLK CENTER
The Smokehouse at the Ozark Folk Center
1032 Park Avenue
Mountain View, AR 72560
(870) 269-3851
www.OzarkFolkCenter.com
Fried pies, chocolate peanut butter pie
North central

SKINNY J'S
205 South Main Street
Jonesboro, AR 72401
(870) 275-6264

www.facebook.com/pages/Skinny-Js/119280161507514
Pecan fried pie
Delta/northeast

SKYLINE CAFÉ
618 Mena Street
Mena, AR 71953
(479) 394-5152
Southwest

SMOKEY JOE'S BBQ
824 Military Road
Benton, AR 72015
(501) 315-8333
www.SmokeyJoesBenton.com
Central

SNAPPY'S
11111 U.S. 65 S
Bee Branch, AR 72013
(501) 654-2285
Fried pies
Northwest

SOUTH END GRILL
2121 Batesville Road
Batesville, AR 72501
(870) 251-2229
Peanut butter meringue pie
Delta/north central

THE STATION CAFÉ
111 North Main Street
Bentonville, AR 72712
(479) 273-0553
Walnut pie
Northwest

STOBY'S
405 West Parkway
Russellville, AR 72801
(479) 968-3816
805 Donaghey Avenue
Conway, AR 72034
(501) 327-5447
www.stobys.com
Possum pie
West

STONEBROOK FUDGE FACTORY
101 East Main
Mountain View, AR 72560
(501) 269-5955
Fried pies
North central

STUBBY'S BBQ
3024 Central Avenue
Hot Springs, AR 71913
(501) 620-4596
www.StubbysBBQ.com
Fried pies
Southwest

SUE & CAROL'S
938 North Stateline Road
Texarkana, AR 71854
(870) 774-0859
Southwest

SUE'S KITCHEN
524 S Church Street
Jonesboro, AR 72401
(870) 972-6000
Pink lemonade pie
Delta/northeast

SUSAN'S RESTAURANT
1440 West Sunset Avenue
Springdale, AR 72764
(479) 751-1445
Various pies
Northwest

SWEET TREATS
5 Main Street
Lamar, AR 72846
(479) 647-0133
www.facebook.com/greg.heiser.lamar
Caramel pecan pie, possum pie
West

T AND T DINER
20394 Sonora Acres Road
Springdale, AR 72764
(479) 751-4797
Northwest

TERRY'S FINER RESTAURANT
5018 Kavanaugh Boulevard
Little Rock, AR 72207
(501) 663-4152
www.facebook.com/TerrysFinerFoodsTheRestaurant
Apple tartine
Central

THAT PLACE CAFÉ
88 North Centennial Avenue
West Fork, AR 72774
(479) 839-2234
Northwest

THREE SAM'S BARBEQUE JOINT
10508 Mann Road
Mabelvale, AR 72103
(501) 407-0325
Peanut butter pie
Central

TJ'S PLACE
1385 California Avenue Southwest
Camden, AR 71701
(870) 837-1707
Southwest

TRIO'S
8201 Cantrell Road #100
Little Rock, AR 72227
(501) 221-3330
www.triosrestaurant.com
Raspberry cream cheese pie
Central

VILLAGE WHEEL
1400 Central Boulevard
Bull Shoals, AR 72619
(870) 445-4414
Strawberry rhubarb pie
North central

VIOLA STAMPEDE
9740 U.S. 62 West
Viola, AR 72583
(870) 458-2112
Coconut cream pie
North central

Coconut cream pie at Viola Stampede in Viola. *Kat Robinson*.

WAGON WHEEL RESTAURANT
166 South Broadview
Greenbrier, AR 72058
(501) 679-5009
Meringue pies
Central

WHITE PIG INN
5231 East Broadway
North Little Rock, AR 72117
(501) 945-5551
www.WhitePigInn.com
Fried pies
Central

WINK'S DAIRY BAR
2900 East Washington Avenue
North Little Rock, AR 72114
(501) 945-9025
Coconut meringue pie
Central

THE WOODEN SPOON
1021 South Gentry Boulevard
Gentry, AR 72734
(479) 736-3030
www.WoodenSpoonGentry.com
Northwest

WOOD'S PLACE
1137 State Highway 4B
Camden, AR 71701
(870) 836-0474
Southwest

YOUR MAMA'S GOOD FOOD
221 West Second Street
Little Rock, AR 72201
(501) 372-1811
www.YourMamasGoodFood.com
Pecan pie
Central

ZOE'S
2230 Malvern Avenue #H
Hot Springs, AR 71901
(501) 321-2921
Lemon French coconut pie
Southwest

Index

About the Author

K at Robinson is a food and travel writer based in Little Rock. She still travels Arkansas and the South searching for good stories, tall tales and the next great little restaurant, but now she's also communications manager for the Arkansas Department of Parks and Tourism. Not that there's anything wrong with that.

Her credits include life as the "Eat Arkansas" girl for the *Arkansas Times*, an eight-year stint producing Today's THV *This Morning* (CBS Little Rock), three years producing for KAIT-TV in Jonesboro and a college career in novelty music radio.

Kat is a featured blogger with Lonely Planet, an explorer with *Arkansas Wild*, a hamburger and sweets correspondent for Serious Eats and an occasional contributor to publications both inside and outside Arkansas. In the past she's been a bi-weekly columnist with *Sync Weekly*, an adventurer for *2njoy Magazine*, a writer for *Deep South Magazine*, an eco-conscious journalist for *GreenZine*, a mommy blogger for *Savvy Kids* and a contributor to *Food Network Magazine*. Kat's work has also appeared in *Little Rock Family Magazine*,

Living in Arkansas Emerald City of the South and the print version of the *Arkansas Times*, as well as the *Arkansas Free Press*, *Let's Go Magazine* and *Today's Man*. Her latest work has included *Forbes Travel Guide's* Startle.com, *USA Today* and *Cat Fancy*. She was recognized by the Arkansas Department of Parks and Tourism in 2011 with a Henry Award for Media Support; with the 2011 award for Best Freelance Writing for a Large Daily by the Arkansas Press Association; and numerous times by the *Arkansas Times* as a runner-up for Best Local Blog (behind the *Times*'s own "Arkansas Blog").

Kat lives with her daughter, Hunter, in her hometown of Little Rock. Her interests include historical food research, highway history and amateur photography. She continues to blog at her personal website, TieDyeTravels. com, and also blogs for the Arkansas Department of Parks and Tourism at TravelArkansas.com.

About the Photographer

G rav Weldon is a freelance photographer and digital medium artist living in the hills of northwest Arkansas with his books and cats. His work can be found in *Cat Fancy*, *Arkansas Wild* and numerous other publications.

Visit us at
www.historypress.net